A Blueprint for the Regulation of Artificial Intelligence Technologies

By

Frank Wolf

A Blueprint for the Regulation of Artificial Intelligence Technologies

By Frank Wolf

This book first published 2022

Ethics International Press Ltd, UK

British Library Cataloguing in Publication Data

A catalogue record for this book is available from the British Library

Print Book ISBN: 978-1-871891-73-7

eBook ISBN: 978-1-871891-74-4

ACKNOWLEDGEMENT

The reader is undoubtedly familiar with book acknowledgments and may have noticed similarities among them. These similarities refer to the authors' painful and lonely labor of word-smithery, neglected spouses who soldiered through this ordeal, children who suffered greatly from the lack of attention and whose development may have been temporarily impaired. This is duly noted. Additionally, the author recognizes Ethics Press International, its publisher Sarah Palmer, and editor Amanda Briggs, for sharing the need to establish ethical standards.

CONTENTS

FOREWORD: ANNOTATED TABLE OF CONTENTS

1 Welcome to Industrial Revolutions

The first chapter sets the stage for understanding how new technologies fit into history. Artificial Intelligence invades people's lives, motivated perhaps by good intentions but having possibly bad outcomes. What are our defenses and responses? First, we do not have to invent an entirely new ethic regime for the 4th industrial revolution. We should start by looking back. Aristotle told us that rule-based reasoning leads to good decisions, which clearly defines machine learning. The second is to recall how Artificial Intelligence became a discipline; it was discovered and defined by private initiatives from academia and industry. It happened through personal leadership from John McCarthy, Marvin Minsky, Claude Shannon, and others. Private enterprises are needed again. Selected ideas from DaVinci, Hobbes, Descartes, Hume, and Mills can guide Artificial Intelligence ethics today. A Dartmouth-type conference would be a good start, a digital Breton Woods even better on a larger scale.

2 Which Ethical Framework? Pick one!

There are many regulators with a legitimate mandate to regulate. Many others love to control and see their agenda expressed in the form of guidelines. The candidates are GDPR General Data Protection Regulation; OECD Organization of Economic Development; EC European Commission; The White House; CCPA California Consumer Privacy Act; G-20 the 19+1, EU countries; UN the United Nations; the COE Council of Europe; the WTO World Trade Organization; ITU International Telecommunication Union, and many more. The GDPR and the State of California have unsynchronized privacy enforcement rules, which are challenging to comply with for international firms.

3 Role Models for Self-Regulation already exist

Self-regulation, contrary to popular views, does not mean selfish or self-serving. For this discussion, the term "self" implies taking responsibility for constructive outcomes. An entity that self-regulates can be a person, a group of persons, a corporate entity for profit or not for profit, but it cannot be a part of a government. One such example is FINRA, the Financial Industry Regulatory Authority overseeing the securities market. It is a self-regulating government corporation without being part of the US government itself. Complying with its extensive rules is a condition for trading securities. ISO, the International Organization for Standardization, certifies voluntary member corporations for compliance with standards of quality. That compliance certification, like ISO-9000, creates market value for companies and falls under the rubric of ethics.

4 The Case for Starting with Self-Regulation First

This chapter supports private initiatives to lead public ones in more detail. Both are essential! Adopting ethical standards for new technology is not a game of winning and losing. Workable ethics standards are best crafted on-field experience and then translated into precision domain-specific legislation. Given the complexity of Artificial Intelligence, merely seeking a common denominator of values is insufficient in most cases. Practical experience brings out the best in all instances, as public/private cooperation is ultimately required. In this case, self and then co-regulation between the private- and public sectors will reasonably assure AI's control remains in human hands. The private sector speaks through two non-governmental organizations (NGOs) and cooperates with governmental oversight. One NGO to self-regulate its corporate members, and the other is to handle abuse by being an ombudsman seeking settlement of disputes. In summary, self-regulation establishes ethical rules leading to co-regulation and enforcement. This chapters' discussion covers techno-hype, creating common values, accountability, and considering risk/ benefit for humans.

5 What to Regulate, that is the Ethics Question

This chapter discusses historical ethics values to guide Artificial Intelligence technology in its quest for standards today. Rather than absolutes, this chapter starts with considering concepts like conscience and conscientiousness to separate good from evil, the rights of natural persons for the digital right to be forgotten and even remembered; humans have callings to fulfill, and those come with obligations and with errors to correct promptly. Unique technology-based rights issues arise from equity, limits and boundaries, and entitlements to explained decisions. Technology at some future point may even consider wisdom and beneficence as primary objectives.

6 Ethics Self-Regulation in Practice

This chapter is about the How-To for building ethics into the technology of Artificial Intelligence. The word "technology" emphasizes that this chapter is not about a company or an industry and not even an economic sector. It is about AI-related technologies, ethics issues, and how we handle them now! Referenced organizations like the AAAI, IEEE, ISO, ACM, and OpenAI are influential. Their objectives, organization, products, and services, plus funding and governance, are detailed. In the end, Chapter 6 looks at looming conflicts like these: a) private- v public regulation, b) now, later, or never regulation, or (c) kicking the can down the road and (d) machine-learned human judgment algorithms that pretend to conform to good ethics rules all the time.

7 Re-Engineering Our Common Future

One cannot expect that the past will exactly repeat itself. However, one can look back to observe how society responded when challenged and how those challenges led to legislation. The events that led to creating The Occupational Safety and Health Organization (OSHA) started with the problem of unacceptably dangerous working conditions. With the benefit of private initiatives to reduce such risk, legislation followed. The implication is that similar paths may evolve to address technologies related to Artificial Intelligence.

8 Measuring Ethics

If we don't measure ethics, we will never know if we have any! This chapter introduces the measurability of ethics and how it may fit into the NGO approach for this new technology. Simple techniques include discussion diagrams and the well documented Triple Bottom Line (TBL) which is originally an accounting method for profit, people and planet.

9 The Next Level – Quantum Computing

Artificial Intelligence is here, but it has not reached its pinnacle yet. Quantum computing may be here soon to help Artificial Intelligence get there. And when it does, humankind may experience progress in curing several diseases. Criminal persons, criminal companies- and criminal governments may celebrate the cracking of crypto security codes to steal money from treasuries worldwide. After a layman's description of the term "quantum," the chapter addresses the need for ethical standards arising from the distribution and ownership of new tools and information. Quantum computing and Artificial Intelligence share the urgent need of being controlled by people and for people.

10 Regulatory Challenges

A co-regulatory ethics regime presumes a buy-in from the public- and private sources. It is not a foregone conclusion that governments and industries trust each other sufficiently to work together well. Challenges arise when former models get updated with new data or used for different purposes. This chapter explores model risks, data governance, integration, and access to technology. One can expect the industry to challenge governments for money and for control. That is the case in both democracies and dictatorships, and increasing concentration of capital in private hands, rather than government, is a contributing cause.

11 Regulatory Trends

The next to last chapter has a message of hope. For the long term, the trend maybe towards ethics basics to be established and mostly observed. Cooperation in corporate taxation among the rich democracies may lead to similar collaboration for rules in Artificial Intelligence ethics. But in technology terms, criminals are faster than police chiefs. Many imbalances to keep artificial Intelligence under democratic human control will continue to exist. Conflicts can arise from the self-serving large corporations with revenues greater than the budget of nations. Endless AI opportunities will create persistent ethical issues in different domains. Countries do claim sovereignty and do things to which the international community objects. In the future, perhaps corporate caring will be part and parcel of financial optimizations. As the industry challenges world governments for control of technology, the best way to accommodate this trend is to offer the industry a seat at the governing table, at the UN for example.

12 Fourteen Points

On January 19th, 1919, Woodrow Wilson, the 28th President of the United States, introduced 14 Points at the Versailles Peace Conference. One of those points was the right to self-determination. Self-determination, in this case, refers to nations and their unique cultures, languages, and history. It resonated at the beginning of the 20th Century with an exhausted world population awaking to the decline of colonialism. While Wilson's ultimate League of Nations project failed, some ideas prevailed and now live in the United Nations.

The Fourth Industrial Revolution, which includes the technologies of Artificial Intelligence, is coming fast and furiously. Its effect on society will be as existential as was the settlement of WWI. Unlike the people during WWI, we in the 21st Century are not exhausted and have the means to prepare for better outcomes. The analogy is this: Wilsons' 14 Points resonated with nations and created hope for global peace, although it ultimately did not deliver peace. The 14 points in this chapter may resonate with the current business- and government leaders and provide a means for balance.

Fourteen is just a number. Wilson's fourteen were guideposts for a new world. These fourteen are guideposts for a new technology.

PROLOGUE

Artificial Intelligence is here, and one cannot escape it; too late!
It is ubiquitous, fast, and we are not sure where it is going.
It is unregulated; there are no ethics standards yet.
It feels like the 4th Industrial Revolution is here.
Time is of the essence to control this.
Could we be doomed?
Probably not!
At risk
yes

Can we handle it, and if so, how best? That is the core question this book explores. Society has adjusted to past existential changes when confronted with the steam engine, mass production, and digital technologies. Let us assume we can do it again and learn, adjust, and thrive with Artificial Intelligence on our side. The goal is to keep this technology under human control at all costs because the trends point in the direction of profound societal changes in how we live, how we work, and how we relate to each other as neighbors and as nations. The process to settle on meaningful ethical standards now will set the stage for the big existential one to come next.

The proposed mechanism to implement ethical Artificial Intelligence standards is through two non-governmental organizations. The first NGO, a corporate membership type, develops AI ethics operating standards based on case law. Its corporate members commit to observing domain-specific ethics standards, thereby creating public trust and reputational value for themselves and their shareholders. However, one-size ethics does not fit all domains. For example, rules in pharmaceutical cases are different from those for consumer credit. Rule-writing legislators would lack the precision for incorporating all possible considerations into one general piece of legislation. Nonetheless, standards emerging from practice will have credibility in the eyes of the public and be plausible. The second NGO, a grant-funded institution, advocates for the prevention of abuse in Artificial Intelligence. It is likely to be a public service operation similar to Oxfam or The Better Business Bureau. In combination, those two NGOs cover the willing- and the unwilling in Artificial Intelligence ethics. Both need to be legally independent of each other, and both will support evolving self-regulation and co-regulation. As a result of these initiatives, society can realistically expect continuously improving ethics standards for this technology. Hoping for perfect ethics standards that are fit for any given point in time is probably unrealistic.

So why is there such an urgency to establish rules? For one thing, this technology is everywhere and advancing fast. At the same time, its hope and hype are ill-understood in many quarters. Individuals, companies, and even competing nations do have incentives to act morally wrong through this technology. Furthermore, self-regulation is not as radical an idea as it may seem in this instance. Self-regulation has a positive precedent in ISO standards for product quality and services. It is noteworthy that achieving quality is both good ethics and also good business. Past attempts to self-regulate have been called self-serving, and such attempts have thus failed to make a big difference. That in itself is not sufficient reason not to do it better this time around! The current business climate is tilting towards a softer form of capitalism that supports self-regulation. Embracing symbiosis, as observed in the natural world, is the metaphor. Even Beneficence is not too much to ask for, as accounting for people, profit, and planet are happening already. Pure competition produces a few clear winners and many losers, while cooperative governance creates a far more significant number of winners.

Future NGO-derived ethics standards will most likely have undergone thoughtful evaluations before adoption. Even though a group of compliance officers and ethicists may achieve neutrality, they are nevertheless humans and, by definition, fallible. Linking Artificial Intelligence ethics to global ethics classics can further substantiate the arguments. For example, take Aristotle's idea that living within good rules leads to good decisions. Machine learning, after all, is all about finding good rules by which to live. Similarly, Thomas Hobbs said that the State is not above the law. In recognition technologies, for example, that theoretically means the rules that apply to corporations are the same as those used by law enforcement. David Hume's counsel tells us to rely on experiences more than reasoning? Spot on! Theories in Utilitarianism, or more specifically John Stuart Mills' works, are often referenced in the Artificial Intelligence literature because it aims to make people happy.

NGO-derived ethics standards will also have to fit into concepts such as wisdom and common sense, conscience, callings and rights, accountability, agency, dignity, explanations, monopoly, and causality, and more. Formal guidance comes from many quarters like the GDPR, OECD, the European Commission, the White House, the State of California, the G-20, the United Nations and its ITU, the Council of Europe, and the World Trade Organization. The GDPR and the State of California issue rules; the rest only advise, which is a lot easier.

What is the next step? Artificial Intelligence became a discipline after an historic conference at Dartmouth College in 1956 when organizations like IBM and universities like MIT and others took the initiative to define it. This technology now needs another forum like that to establish the rules for it. Leading institutions have the opportunity to lead again and make this technology fit for serving people. To self-regulate, in this case, means ethical leadership by being an example and coincidentally creating public trust. Co-regulating sets the stage for a softer form of governance. It balances financial optimization with human caring, national sovereignty with globalization, and protects the natural person's right to live free from threats and degradation.

The need for the establishment of ethical standards is also a call for technological leadership in general. As the technology moves faster than regulators can write the rules, narrowing the growing ethics gap becomes feasible. Lets' go for it!

The last chapter offers fourteen suggestions (points) to guide this call for action. These points are fashioned after US President Woodrow Wilson's 14 Fourteen Points from the 1919 Versailles Peace Conference, tweaked towards applied ethics.

CHAPTER 1
WELCOME TO INDUSTRIAL REVOLUTIONS

If the technological trends we are currently facing amount to a 4th industrial revolution, let us remember that humanity has survived the first three, namely those of steam engines, mass production, and digital information technologies. If *We The People,* that is you the reader, me the author and all humanity of this planet presume that we can rest assured that all will survive as well, and then do nothing, we are in trouble. In the absence of action, *We The People* may find ourselves aimlessly wandering in the jungle of a new technology. We have to make decisions that support life; and we have to make decisions that avoid taking away from life.

The new challenge is how to prosper under revolution #4 and keep those technologies, including Artificial Intelligence, under human control. Surprisingly, some tools for ethics control may come from both ancient philosophy and from modern organizational management. The consequence of failing, that is, not keeping artificial intelligence under human control, is not good; think bad actors pulling all the strings! Human subservience to this technology can innocently happen in at least two different ways. First, it can happen as John Doe willingly trades personal responsibility for convenience and lives a happy life being a serf. Second, it can occur when one or more large corporations with more power and money than nations manipulate the economy for their benefit. This includes the cast of current dictators in the world and some celebrity chief executives as well.

The research question is how to operationalize AI ethics, however small initially, but quickly, as the technology moves faster than the sheriff. This inquiry started with a few academic papers and is now a book. It makes a case for corporate co-regulation as a precursor to inevitable legislation in the USA and the EU. Ethical building blocks come from established philosophy. Take Aristotle's idea that living by good rules leads to good decisions. Linked to todays' artificial intelligence algorithms, it is what any neural network hopes to do. The ethical question is, when are rules good?

Similarly, Thomas Hobbs found that the State is not above the law, which applies to how far facial recognition in the hands of law-enforcements is allowed to go. Rene Descartes recognized that we could employ the language of mathematics to specify ethical objectives, as in Python programming to facilitate machine-ethics. Then David Hume told us to rely on experiences more than reasoning; an idea that supports machine learning! The philosophy of Unilateralism addresses human well-being. Happiness is spot-on for good artificial intelligence itself. Three cheers for John Stuart Mills, artificial intelligence does indeed aim to serve humankind with beneficence. Under a philosophical umbrella, we consider wisdom, conscience, callings, and the rights enshrined in the fundamental law. With artificial intelligence technology in mind, one adds accountability, agency, dignity, explained decisions, jobs and society, data monopoly, and causality (hopefully not justified entirely by correlation). There is no shortage of guidelines from entities with regulatory ambition: GDPR, OECD, the European Commission, the White House, the State of California, the G-20, the United Nations and its ITU, the Council of Europe, and the World Trade Organization are vocal examples. None except the GDPR and California have any direct authority to regulate.

Whether voluntarily or eventually mandated, the responsibility and liability for complying with ethical standards lie with the creators and operators of artificial intelligence technology. This is easier said than done as there are no standards yet.

Good fortune has it that co-regulatory role models already exist, namely ISO for quality and FINRA for trust in the field of finance. The International Organizations for Standards (ISO) is a Geneva-based independent, not-for-profit, non-governmental membership organization operating in 164 countries. Of particular relevance to Artificial Intelligence are the ISO quality standards series 9000 for products and services, and 14000 on environmental issues, plus ISO - IEC 27001 on information security management. Here, *quality* for products and services is not a product specification as might be expected! Instead, process quality infers product quality! Taking a hint from ISO, one may conclude ethics standards from co-regulated procedures lead to ethical outcomes. ISO quality certifications do have value for the holders. Certified artificial intelligence ethics certification may similarly confer trust as long as humans remain in collective control.

The Financial Industry Regulatory Authority (FINRA) exists to protect investors. It regulates its member broker-dealers, their employees, and customers. FINRA, although authorized by the US Congress, is not part of the US government. It is a not-for-profit government corporation and is self-regulatory/co-regulatory with complex rules members are obliged to follow.

This book's suggested mechanism to implement ethical AI standards calls for two non-governmental organizations. The first, a corporate membership NGO, develops AI ethics operating standards based on historic human values. Specific rules evolve from cases unique to industrial sectors and are therefore acceptable to most corporate members. The second, a non-membership NGO to advocate for the prevention of AI ethics abuse. It may take its role model from Oxfam and join a confederation of like-minded entities. Both the first and the second NGOs have to operate as independent legal entities, but both will support co-regulation of artificial intelligence ethics. The first is membership funded, and the second is to be financed by public service grants. Both support co-regulation for pending legislation affecting technology.

What is the next step? Artificial Intelligence became a discipline after an historic conference at Dartmouth College in 1956 when corporations like IBM and universities like MIT took the initiative to deal with artificial intelligence, a new technology. Said technology now needs an ethical grounding, and leading corporations and great universities are called upon to rise to the cause of stipulating safe artificial intelligence for humans. Initial co-regulation, in this case, means continuously leading by example in which case ethical AI will win by market acceptance. Inevitable ethics violators will be dealt with via NGO # 2 first, and then by enforcement of eventual legislation later. The result is viewed as continuously improving ethics, supported by multitude of interests, benefiting humans, who remain in charge. Without a measurement regime for ethics in Artificial Intelligence, unfortunately, progress remains vague, and society may end up somewhere else. Well – established rules a la Aristotle can be measured. The tools for doing that exists, and can be adjusted to fit a new need, in the form of Triple Bottom Line accounting and the United Nations promoted moral rules of Sustainability, for example. For the urgent need to establish-and enforce ethical standards in new technologies the tools are there and the willpower to do it has to be found.

This book is about the anticipation of good tidings for humans resulting from Artificial Intelligence. The discussion includes the details to ascertain good outcomes. Adjustments to this new world will be substantial, and it will require all of us to adapt. But how? We live in a dangerously contentious world. The answer to the problem is a cocktail of good old-fashioned human affairs management, ranging from regulation, co-regulation, self-governance, adhering to democracy, a relatively free market, and learning from history, to mention a few hints.

To start the process for our new future, lets us graphically find out where we are: Graphically, you, the reader, can find your spot on the chart below just by identifying with one of the statements:

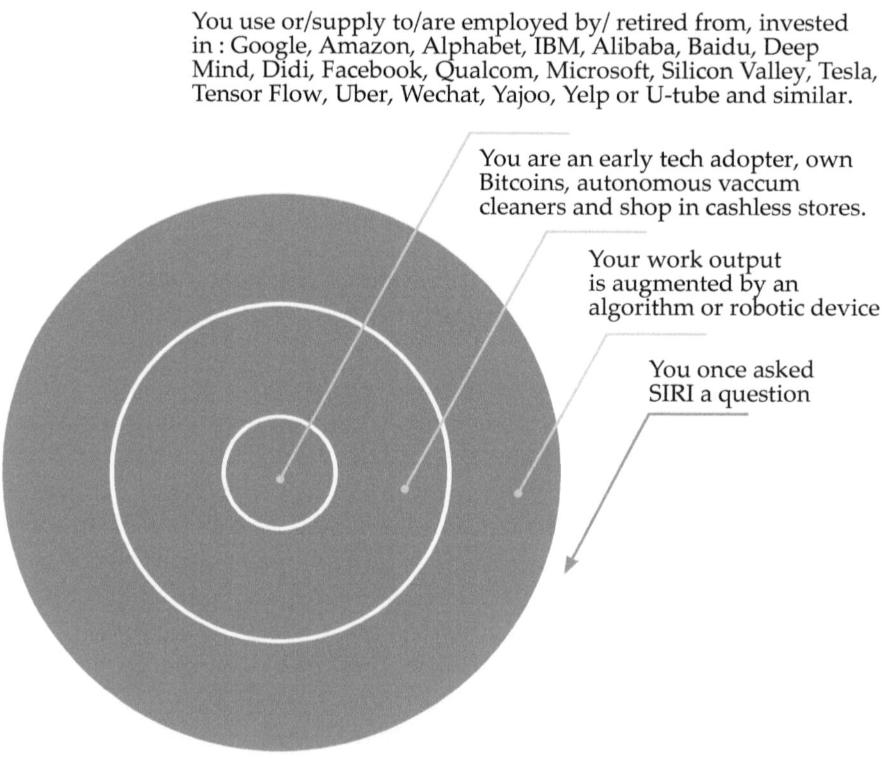

Figure 1.1

The probability is high that all of us have a role of relevance in the future.

Our collective industrial future implies a looming existential change. The literature immodestly referred to this as The Fourth Industrial Revolution, or 4IR for short. Fundamental changes in how we work and live will be the result of our adaption to Artificial Intelligence. Keep in mind that nobody knows! Think of the prior three industrial revolutions to grasp the magnitude of what was in store:

The steam engine (1790 – 1830), which powered transportation and agriculture.

Electricity (1870 – 1914), which powered sciences and technology, and infrastructure.

Electronic data (1950 -), which poweredwhich powered us, personally and literally.

The time to address Artificial Intelligence is now because it will change the way we work and live. It will change how we relate to one another or whether we relate to each other at all. Artificial Intelligence can be incredible and liberating for humans and also very limiting at the same time.

This book aims to meet several current needs: The first is to keep this technology under human control. The worst case is to prevent humans from becoming automatons, which is every dictators' dream. People who claim to know what comes next are called futurists. Several have appeared before, and an appropriate example is a book by E. M. Forster called "The Machine Stops," published in 1909. This book's second purpose is to build public trust in Artificial Intelligence and technology to thrive and deliver benefits to people. Lack of confidence is a problem for every business using AI and for every authority trying to regulate it. The third purpose of the book is urgency. The rate of technological progress could become humankind's road to serfdom, a borrowed expression from a book by F.D. Hayek. Previous industrial revolutions had a run-up time of almost 100 years before reaching maturity. This coming revolution is likely to be much quicker in establishing itself. Once established, undesirable aspects of 4IR may be irreversible. Last but not least the purpose of this book is to show the way for getting control done!

It all started around 350 BC

History matters as ignoring it may lead to repeating it, according to popular wisdom. In this case, the history of human ethics is exceptionally long and rich, while Artificial Intelligence is too young to have ethical standards. We find ourselves at the beginning of what may turn out to become the 4th Industrial Revolution; what would the next generations write about us? Did we manage this technology to be beneficial to all people? Did we learn anything from past human struggles, or were we neglectful and enabled dictators and oligarchs to turn us into programmed automatons? A thoughtful design of regulation and self-regulation is the essence of this work. Rather than dictating what that design is to be, collective and collaborative thinking must ultimately address ethics concerns.

This discussion of ethics in artificial intelligence has a foundation in the customs of Western cultures and values. Although other cultures have ethics as well, they are both different and similar in many respects. With a specific emphasis on Artificial Intelligence, the prime thinkers are:

- Aristotle (384-322 BC) — Stipulated that rule-based reasoning leads to the right decisions; modern AI algorithms are rule based decision making.

Aristotle taught in the Lyceum by introducing syllogisms, which are the rules. With a bit of imagination, we can think of syllogisms being the modern equivalent to computer code by which language Python, for instance, is rule-based.

- Leonardo Da Vinci (1452-1519) — Designed a computing machine, albeit only on paper; quantum computers, still living in laboratories, will help Artificial Intelligence penetrate deeper into data.

Da Vinci designed a computing machine with 13 registers, the same type of registers we find in modern digital computers, only that now there are many more of them. Computing capacity is a critical ingredient for artificial intelligence to work in daily life. If a computer takes one week to define the next move in a chess game, it is not playable. Quantum computing is on the horizon, and it is fundamentally different from its digital cousin.

- Thomas Hobbes (1588-1679) — The rule of law applies to persons and the state; autonomous vehicles must obey all traffic laws, that is, the applicable ethics rule.

Hobbes was a political philosopher who advocated for a solid central governmental authority, the King. Having lived 91 years is evidence that the King did not object to his views. Hobbs also found similarities between human reasoning and the field of mathematics because humans often add and subtract and make calculations before reaching conclusions. The parallel here lies in the quantitative nature of artificial intelligence.

- Rene Descartes (1596-1650) — maintained that rationality and reason is expressible through mathematics; objectives can be in the form of equations, thereby implying rationality.

In the field of mathematics, Rene Descartes connected geometry and algebra at the time. In philosophy, he made the connection from the human soul to the human body. A more mysterious connection to Artificial Intelligence is between robots and their hypothetical future self-awareness and free will. That would imply a machine with a soul.

- David Hume (1711-1776) —A Scottish philosopher and essayist said that human knowledge comes from experience rather than reason. Deep-learning and neural networks learn from cause-effect relationships suggested by data.

Hume said that principles of induction, or learning, come from repeated exposures. His writings include a treatise of human nature, human understanding, and principles of morals. For the current generation, these ethical rules suggest extracting knowledge from data under ethical principles.

- John Stuart Mill (1806 – 1873) was a British philosopher, political economist, and civil servant best known for Utilitarianism as defined by the book with that title (1863). Utilitarianism centers on the Greatest Happiness Principle, which principle is spot-on congruent with today's justification of Artificial Intelligence itself., namely, seeking humans' well-being. J.S. Mill's philosophy weighs decisions in terms of quantifying gain v pain. These rules fit Artificial Intelligence well because (a) they are rational, and rationality is a percept in this technology, and (b) they pertain to individual human decisions, plus, (c) a basis for separating moral right-and-wrong. J.S. Mill must have sensed back in the 19th century what was coming down the pike to graciously enrich this generation with this insight. Quoting from chapter 2, "What is there to decide whether a particular pleasure is worth purchasing at the cost of specific pain?

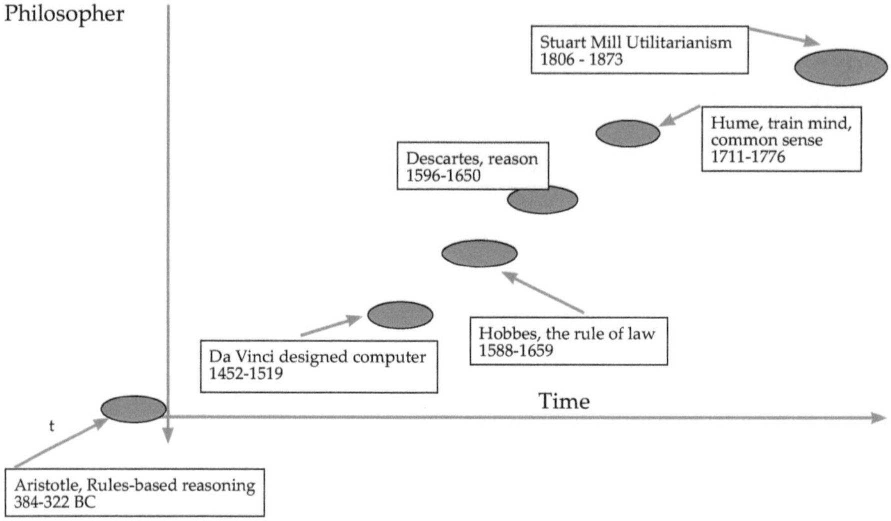

Figure 1.2 *Western Ethics time line*

The nature of industrial revolutions

When we think of revolutions, what comes to mind are violent political overthrows of an old regime in favor of a new ideology. Examples are the French Revolution (1789), undoing a monarchy in favor of liberty, equality, and brotherhood; the Soviet Revolution to replace the Czar with Communism (1917); and the American Revolution (1775), ending British colonialism in North America. Industrial revolutions share that overthrow feature of replacing the old with the new only in terms of technology. The much nicer term "creative destruction" was coined by Joseph Schumpeter in 1942. The term refers to innovation and creativity being an enduring part of capitalism, fostering an ongoing internal renewal. Creative destruction does not rise to the level of a revolution since it often is limited to only replace one mouse trap with a better one.

In the past, humankind has survived industrial revolutions, such as steam power, electricity, the introduction of the power loom and the spinning jenny (circa 1770), which enabled the global cotton market, the telegraph and telephone, the internal combustion engine, sewing machines, supermarkets and all that goes with them. This Artificial Intelligence revolution promises to be faster and more profound than previous ones because its building blocks, such as data, computers, and potential applications, are in place on a large scale.

Technological revolutions share the *overthrow* aspect, without people's discontent not necessarily being the cause. Technological revolutions are the result of creative people tinkering and subsequently making discoveries that serve human needs. For instance, Gutenberg's (1440) discovery of the moveable printing process led to the distribution of information, literature, science, and scholarship and the growth of publishing as an industry. It was the technological revolution of agriculture when around 1868, Fritz Haberman discovered that applying chemical fertilizers increases food production yields. It led to the support of larger populations, longer lifespans for humans, and economic growth. The ability to split the atom, shown by Rutherford (1917), introduced a new branch of physics, and 30 years later, the atomic bomb by Oppenheimer and his team ended World War II in the Pacific and producing much electricity since then. We face the start of a potential fourth industrial revolution. It builds on the cornerstones of the previous three, steam engine, electricity, and digital computing.

Optimists looking back argue that steam power revolutionized transportation and replaced many horses, but horses morphed into pets, and now there are even more. Optimists can also say that electricity enabled cities to grow and enabled the move from farming to manufacturing without replacing farms. Equally, optimists argue that digital computing enabled a service industry to evolve, employing many people under better working conditions than before. The possible fourth industrial revolution may bring about many fundamental changes in how we live and work, the details of which remain relatively unknown. But understanding where we are in the revolutionary cycle can make an enormous difference. Here both self-regulation and regulations can steer human destiny in the right direction

A short history of Artificial Intelligence

The term "Artificial Intelligence" implies machine-generated, human-like thinking and decision making. A decision where (a) human-like thinking includes learning, problem-solving, decision-making in that sequence, and (b) rational acting machines doing human tasks a bit better. Rationality is technically defined as human-like acting based on logic, even though humans tend to occasionally drop rationality and become emotional instead, in which case we do not want machines actually to learn that. As long as machines have no self-awareness, they mimic human weirdness, which can be a problem. In practice, we envision having computing machines that can perceive via sensing devices, apply reasoning based on learned logic, and then act rationally in real-time. For example, we may imagine a little robot crawling along a commercial strawberry field powered by small lithium batteries and equipped with vision capability like the rear-view camera on a car. This little robot can distinguish red from green, and it can examine a strawberry's level of ripeness, then gingerly pick it if warranted, and gently put them into the basket on its back. It will unload at the end of a row and move to an adjacent field and repeat ad-infinitum without breaks or exhaustion. Not even daylight is necessary for this operation. It is a legitimate application of Artificial Intelligence and meets the conditions of both (a) and (b). Ethically, it is benign as it increases productivity, generates more income for the landowners, and relieves humans from back-breaking work for low pay. It also throws low-paid workers doing back-breaking tasks out of work, which has been an age-old problem with any form of automation like the Spinning Jenney in the early industrial revolution. What about the effect on migrant workers it replaces? And their country's dependence on remittances by which many developing countries balance their international payments, enabling critical imports like medicines? It is one of the emerging ethics questions with endless links to social issues. The Boston company who built this cute "*strawberry-picking*" robot is no more ethically responsible than the folks who own the strawberry field in Plantation, Florida. Yet, many of our geographic neighbors in The Bahamas and Central America temporarily face no work – no money – no food.

Finding ourselves at the start of a new and different industrial revolution is sort of exciting. As is the case in all previous industrial processes, that usually is an event and a moment that triggers optimism for a new beginning. For Artificial Intelligence history, it came to be that around anno domini 1956, when a small group of engineers gathered at Dartmouth College to explore the possibility of a future "thinking machine." What led them to *think* so was the availability of data on magnetic tapes, the processing power of machines much more potent than calculators at the time, combined with higher-level programming languages like FORTRAN. All that could lead to computed decisions. Early evidence for a thinking machine concept came out of laboratory experiments in Expert Systems, which had all the elements Artificial Intelligence has today. For example, data comes from sensing a machines' state. Given a specific combination of factors and their respective values, one may draw inferences from that combination. In fact, in the official lingo, this stage of the process was called an "inference engine.". The final step in Expert Systems is a computed recommendation of human quality. Expert Systems' inferences take the form of "what-if-then," which is programable in an expert-system language called "Prolog." The key idea is to transform raw data into information that becomes useful and beneficial for people. The incentive to make Expert Systems in the industry was to train junior workers into experts more quickly, employ fewer experts, and make money above all. In today's business setting, neither the processing logic nor the incentives have fundamentally changed.

We start with raw data in the form of labeled images for face recognition, for example. Then trained software running on super-computers discriminates between cat- or mouse faces. Replace the mouse/cat rule and replace it with human faces, and one can distinguish between friend and foe. The technology of recognizing images is helpful in medicine and national security interpreting orbital photos. It would be good to have standards and rules for bringing out the best of something new and revolutionary as Artificial Intelligence!

CHAPTER 2
WHICH ETHICAL FRAMEWORK? PICK ONE!

We want to find an ethical framework for Artificial Intelligence that has a chance of working in practice and is acceptable and fair or nearly fair to all. One hundred percent agreement is not even the goal for a technology that remains difficult to define.

In a broad sense, the words "Artificial Intelligence" refer to a technology that aims to resemble the cognitive capacity of humans. Allowing ethics to enter is to assure good outcomes just as much as to prevent harmful effects. Dire consequences can be accidental and intentional because the opportunities are so great.

To get a hold on the need for ethics for Artificial Intelligence one must consider that every segment of the world economy has a yet to-be-defined ethics problem. All business activities share data that feeds into computers and, from there, flows into algorithms that assist humans in their work. The tools of the trade are machine learning, natural language processing, computer vision, and robots, among others. Machines now do some of the work humans once did, just as the steam engine replaced horses. The measurement of horsepower is a reminder of that.

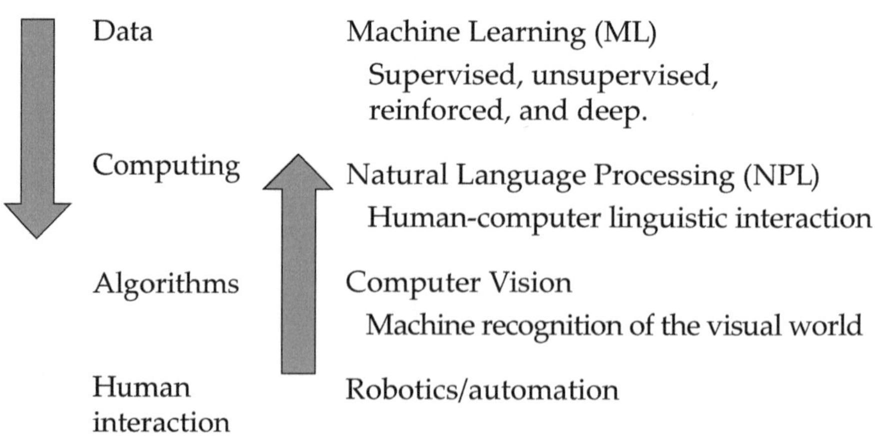

Figure 2.1

Consider the element called "Data" on the left, for example. An average person may define *data* as reams of numbers, words, and letters plus some images and then stop there. But data meticulously organized creates information. Would a fashion designer not be interested in knowledge leading to the understanding of what teenagers are thinking? Economic conditions today are not the same as yesterday. Today data lives in "the cloud" in structured and unstructured formats, the storage of which is cheap. From it, analysts identify patterns and make continuous predictions as data changes. Later in this book, the power of *data* comes up again concerning ethics and privacy. Mobile technologies and digitization create new data quickly and do it massively. The revolutionary aspects of data today are comparable to that of oil last century. Data increases in volume without direct environmental pollution or exhaustion of a natural resource. Data is green! Algorithms are different from conventional software programs. The similarity is that both algorithms and programs live in computing machines. An algorithm continuously learns to perform a task like forecasting the weather, thus producing new information. On the other hand, a computer program only performs a job according to instructions, like next week's payroll calculations. Ethics come into play as soon as a human interaction occurs. Algorithmic applications have their life cycles of birth, adolescence, maturity and, in the end, irrelevance as time moves on. During that cycle, a human must be in charge of data preparation, algorithm testing, explaining, retraining the model, and verifying results, continuously. The commercial world is less than ideal. So good luck with reliable human management of classifications, outliers, and predictions that do not fit correctness of the time. In the absents of ethical norms, humankind is likely to do this poorly. One must realistically expect inefficiencies, foregone opportunities, and risks resulting from faulty conclusions.

Machine Learning (ML) is now a branch of computer science and a recognized field of study. Within ML, "supervised learning" means that the training data has a label by identifying an image as a cat or as not a cat. Once a sufficient number of labeled cat images are on file, the subsequent picture comes with some certainty that it is a cat or not a cat. It follows that the term "unsupervised learning " applies to data that is not labeled. In this instance, a large amount of information leads to an underlying pattern, if one exists. Securities trading data is a case in point as the purpose is to gain a hypothetical advantage. To have an edge is the proverbial name of the game.

Adding to ML's complexity, reinforced learning creates knowledge from trial and error while looking for the desired conclusion. Programmed rewards and punishment functions within a model force, or more correctly reinforce, movement into the desired direction. The last variety of ML is "deep learning." Its depth comes from trying to emulate the human brain by building an artificial neural network. In practice, deep learning uses large amounts of disparate data like voice, video, and text. The reader should not stay up all night wondering whether Deep Learning can be supervised, unsupervised, or reinforced; it can!

Regulators – an alphabet soup

Regulation is necessary. Being a regulator can also be fun because regulators get to tell people what to do without being accountable for the eventual outcome down the road. Writing the rules is also necessary and fun because of the imposition of penalties for non-compliance. Even better, while compliance is essential, enforcing regulation can be very profitable for the legal profession by focusing on the exceptions to the rules. Apply that logic to the technology of Artificial Intelligence and what comes to mind is the expression "Houston; we have a problem." Regulation is cumbersome and slow-moving, while this technology is ubiquitous and moving faster than past industrial revolutions in our history. Projecting that scenario into the near future, and what must regulators get right?

Therefore, it is not surprising that many regulatory entities take a public positions and make a great deal of noise to sit on the table of good governance and ethics in Artificial Intelligence. The voices of those in the private sector, those who create, invest, and operate this technology, are relatively quiet and are not sitting at the public table, despite having an important role to play. Both private- and public sectors pursue good governance. So, who are those regulatory parties in the public- and private sectors? The illustrative list includes the following alphabet soup of international regulatory institutions: GDPR, OECD, EC, White House CA, G-20, U.N., Council of Europe, WTO, ITU, and role models for self-regulation like ISO and FINRA.

The technology of Artificial Intelligence is still too undefined, too new, and without precedent to meet court standards. In other words, the technology and its practicing industries are on their own regarding rules for ethics. Self-regulation is a good start and waiting for the law to catch up will lead to more conflicts.

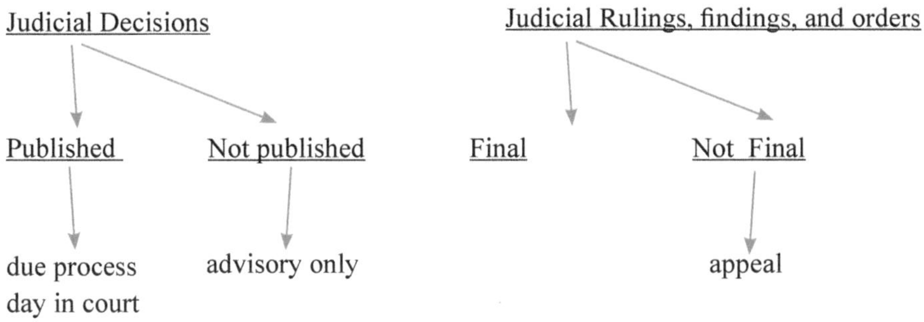

Figure 2.2

The GENERAL DATA PROTECTION REGULATION (GDPR) is a European Union law affecting all citizens within the 28-nation group. To the extent that the rule applies to E.U. citizens outside the E.U., the law is extraterritorial. The law intends to protect the privacy of any natural person, assure that all data collection efforts are lawful, provide a mechanism for data to be erased and forgotten, and ensure that a natural person is not identifiable in databases. It exempts only law enforcement and the military from those restrictions. Protection of the natural person is the ethical principle, while opting in or out of databases is a right. An enhancement to the GDPR is the European e-Privacy Regulation; it is currently in draft form before the European Parliament. This proposed legislation fleshes out practical details to supplement the implementation of the GDPR concerning IoT (the Internet of Things), cookies, and metadata.

THE ORGANIZATION OF ECONOMIC DEVELOPMENT (OECD) is a 36- nation coalition of governments. It issued a 5-points guideline for artificial intelligence applications on May 22, 2019, which is instructive for self-regulation! A guideline is not a regulation, irrespective of who issues it. A guideline says, "accomplish the following," while rules state, "do not do such…". The 5-points OECD guideline is the following:

> Applied Artificial Intelligence should benefit people, planet, drive economic growth and well-being. Note the word "should" in this sentence and understand that this is weak guidance. In other words, let us all be nice!

Artificial Intelligence systems must respect law and human rights rules and support democracy to provide safeguards for a fair society. Similarly, the word "should" is only a suggestion. Also, respect for law and human rights is not a legal option.

Artificial Intelligence should be transparent and understood. In AI-speak, this is called an *explained decision*. Apart from the word "should," this is a fair mandate, albeit not unique. In law, for example, explained judgments are the norm, except under totalitarian regimes. In practice, just because an algorithm suggests a decision, the affected persons may present a challenge and ask why and how.

Artificial Intelligence systems are to be secure and continually evaluated. This expectation is a fair rule under which privacy- and intellectual property is protected. The continuous evaluation provision is also appropriate because technology often starts with good intentions and winds up somewhere else over time. Under the Japanese Just-In-Time management philosophy, "continuous improvement" is fundamental to quality.

Artificial Intelligence developers must be accountable for the outcomes of their works. A better definition of who "developers" are is needed. The British Parliament, for instance, is active in this area. Quoting member Damian Collins MP, "we are facing nothing less than a crisis in our democracy based on the relentless targeting of citizens without their consent by campaigns of disinformation and hate...." The takeaway from this is: (a) early development that from now on data-crime means actual crime, (b) the massive collection of data by a few tech firms is a form of monopoly and by definition illegal, (c) firms that participate on the periphery of ethics like financing or scaping personal profiles off websites to target unsuspecting citizens, are not passive and innocent bystanders.

The EUROPEAN COMMISSION (E.C.) is the executive branch of the European Union. It proposes legislation, implements legislation, and complies with treaties. In 2020 it issued a white paper on Artificial Intelligence emphasizing excellence and trust, where the term "excellence" also suggests and hopes for A.I. leadership by the European Union itself. The article signals the Commissions' intention to regulate well beyond privacy concerns of the GDPR, to regulate

Artificial Intelligence with a focus on liability, risk, record keeping, information accuracy, human oversight, labeling of data from which machines learn, governance, and the future potential of this technology. The paper promotes human-centric ethics and western values. It goes beyond regulation and includes a call for action in developing an industrial capacity. A call for action does not guarantee actions unless it is both funded and thriving.

For the period beyond 2022 the E.C. takes the risk approach in regulating Artificial Intelligence. High risks for people living in Europe are unacceptable. Examples of unacceptable risks are social scoring as in Communist China, threats to water supplies, aspects of automated education, product safety, robotic surgery, and worker selection by algorithms. Low risks are encouraged but still have to meet transparency thresholds. A transparency threshold example is that clients must be aware when communicating with a machine; a machine must identify a deep-fake image. Progress towards functioning regulations includes the E.C.'s submission to the E.U. Parliament for passage and all E.U. states to confirm. The first such regulatory salvo was released in April 2021 for comment. In addition to the above issues, it also addresses biometrics, automated recruitment and transparency in communication.

The WHITE HOUSE (USA) represents the executive branch of the United States, similar to the European Commission (E.C.) does in the European Union (E.U.). The White House issued executive order #13859 in February 2019 that addresses ethics in Artificial Intelligence. It is equally important to understand that these guidelines are just guidelines, not even rules. The guidelines take a sectoral approach and do not recommend a one-size-fists most course because the technology is varied.

The primary audiences are the U.S. government departments, including the Department of Defense (DoD). The document deals with "responsible execution, equity, concern for unintended consequences, traceability of data and justification of outcomes, reliability, and use as originally intended. Guidelines from the executive branch are somewhat binding upon the departments of the U.S. Government itself. It is an excellent first step.

The secondary audience for this order is U.S. commerce. Here the guidelines relate to cost-benefit analysis, risk assessment, integrity, trust, public participation, flexibility, and fairness in the form of non-discrimination. Lose guidelines are not binding for anybody but maybe the first step towards eventual political, time-consuming, and contentious legislation. To solely depend on the cumbersome legislative process for ethics standards in Artificial Intelligence is too risky. The opportunities to build ethics into general contracting, especially government contracting, are not fully explored and hold immense potential. Like self-regulation, government contracting is the practical option to advance Artificial Intelligence ethics now, as well as later. In particular, U.S. Government contract clauses could be a mechanism to enforce ethics in Artificial Intelligence. Gender- and racial non-discrimination should become part and parcel of contracts. Fundamental principles of ethics are part and parcel of government contracts. All one needs to do is establish new standards by doing more.

US Government spending amounted to $ 4.45 T in 2019. The U.S. gross domestic product in 2019 was the U.S. $ 24.45T. That means about 18% of the U.S. output could become more or less compliant with ethical standards on short notice. Ethical standards-setting in this new technology is a worthwhile goal, even though worldwide compliance for it may only be a dream for now. A combination of legislated A.I. standards plus industrial self-regulation must address published guidelines and address ethical standards in general. Such measures are not limited to conscience, rights, callings, wisdom, obligations, limits and boundaries, fairness and equality, potential unintended outcomes, explained decisions, data monopolies. Let us add to the ethics shopping list the concepts of beneficence. The White House and the European Commission are political organizations actively promoting worldwide leadership in Artificial Intelligence technology, a leadership role primarily envisioned for their home turf. There are many crosscurrents between the E.U. and the U.S., but pursuing the goal of ethics standards is no threat to either.

THE STATE OF CALIFORNIA. In the United States, California was the first state to begin data protection by passing the California Consumer Privacy Act (CCPA). It became law in 2018 and took effect in January 2020. This law deals only with protecting consumers' privacy and not Artificial Intelligence in particular. The three pillars of Artificial Intelligence are data, computing, modeling, of with the CCPA addressing data. The new law grants California's consumers the right to know what is collected and grants the option to delete and opt-out of data collection. It applies to businesses in California with more than $25 million in sales, sellers of information handling more than 50,000 consumers, and additional provisions for companies with over 4 million consumers. Other customer service requirements relate to a procedure to opt-out, delete, or "do not sell my info." The current legislative agenda includes Assembly Bill AB-459. It will require the Artificial Intelligence Service Commission to regularly report on State activities relative to automated decisions on appeals and explain their unintended consequences. In a similar vein, AB-459 took effect in February 2021 and offers conventional ethical guidelines for State government agencies to follow.

The takeaway is this: The list of noble intentions contained in the proposed AB-459 qualify their intent by verbs such as to foster, to respond, to ensure, to prioritize, to measure, and to minimize something. While these are welcome first steps in the legislative process, the Bill has to pass two Houses, regulations have to be written and adopted, and appeals are sure to follow. That may take two years or a lot more years. AB-459 allows a long time for the dark forces of malintent to take root.

THE G-20 (Group of 20) is a 19- nation forum of the European Union's central bankers and finance ministers. This group endorsed the OECD's Artificial Intelligence policies by "having regards for" and "recognizing" several key issues such as sustainable development, the importance of Artificial Intelligence, potential benefits and disparate effects, human rights covered under existing constitutions, and embracing opportunities. One must assume that the G-20 will support governmental regulation of Artificial Intelligence congruent with central banking finance policies. Its pronouncements are not binding. Being only a forum, it has no regulatory obligation to fulfill, but its voice is influential.

THE COUNCIL OF EUROPE is a 47-nation member State organization to support democracy and the rule of law in Europe, founded in 1949. The Council of Europe is distinct and separate from the European Council, whose members are the heads of state in the European Union. The Council of Europe focuses on human rights and democracy and has an interest in in developing Artificial Intelligence technologies. The Council takes the role of a consolidator of many ideas from many sources. These sources are conferences in Toronto (2017) on rights and Montreal (2018) on responsibilities. Corporate value statements from Microsoft and Google apply, as do the views from the IEEE, the worlds' largest engineering society. Under the Councils' leadership, representatives from industry, civil society, and governments assemble and debate the coming of Artificial Intelligence and related technologies. While talking does not equate to making rules, talking is constructive in influencing the governance of this technology.

THE UNITED NATIONS is a 193-member nation organization founded in 1945. Its United Nations Educational, Scientific, and Cultural Organization (UNESCO) has joined the debate on Artificial Intelligence with an eye on ethical standards in Artificial Intelligence worldwide. The United Nations does not have the power to write laws, and it cannot impose taxes on members, although it would like to. For example, the Sea (UNCLOS) Law is a treaty more than a law in the traditional sense. Once ratified by U.N. members, it becomes enforceable. While the United States has not ratified UNCLOS, it is abiding by it. An attempt to tax member States with a minuscule fee on international funds transfers to alleviate poverty or fund climate projects was a non-starter. The attempt was called the Tobin Tax. The United Nations' power is thus limited to be a forum and a conscience. UNESCO wants to "guide international actions in the area" of Artificial Intelligence. The way the U.N. does this is by organizing global conferences to air evolving issues and conflicts.

The INTERNATIONAL TELECOMMUNICATIONS UNION (ITU) was founded in 1885 to facilitate worldwide telephone and telegraph communication standards. It is now an agency of the United Nations, and by definition, it is congruent with United Nations' policies. While the United Nations may influence regulation, the ITU is far from directly regulating Artificial Intelligence standards. However, the ITU is perhaps the best neutral platform for ethics standards to evolve from. Like its parent organization, it holds worldwide conferences under the theme "A.I. for Good." As this theme implies, the agency seeks to elevate and promote benefits for people, but the definition of "good" is not a standard.

The WORLD TRADE ORGANIZATION (WTO) is a 164-nation membership organization founded in 1995 to establish stable rules under which trade is enabled and promoted for mutual benefit. Main WTO functions include dispute resolution of trade issues between member nations. Rather than seeking ethics standards for Artificial Intelligence itself, the WTO has taken a narrower approach. The WTO focuses on 3-D printing, Block Chains, and the Internet of Things, also known as "IoT," and related technologies like Augmented Reality. With a focus on broad societal issues. The WTO emphasizes skillset development for the next generation to prevent massive unemployment from automation and Artificial Intelligence-related automation. Regulating ethics standards in trade is peripheral to the WTO's successful mission of dispute settlement. However, dispute settlements may come to a screeching halt if the WTO's case neutrality among its members becomes doubtful. As WTO judges retire at the end of their term and new ones cannot be seated due to membership veto powers, the WTO is potentially declining. Its role as ethics arbiter remains relatively small because it has so many problems of its own.

First, regulators, by definition, are always on the right side of ethics. These advisors aim to assure justice, equity, democracy, and human well-being as viewed from the regulator perch. Secondly, the regulator is rarely responsible for the outcome. Except for the GDPR and the State of California, all the other institutions merely offered "guidelines ." While guidelines are helpful, usually well thought-through, and well-meant, they also tend to be lofty and self-congratulatory without any teeth for enforcement. Remedial actions remain with the practitioners, or their customers, or their victims. Hence, the urgency for standards in artificial intelligence to be promulgated is now. Co- and self-regulating ethics standards have a role to play jointly with women and men of goodwill in commerce worldwide.

CHAPTER 3
ROLE MODELS FOR SELF-REGULATION ALREADY EXIST

At first, when first confronted with the term "self-regulation" in business, a cynic may ask where does self-regulation start and where does self-interest end? The lines do overlap and are therefore blurred. Examples of this conflict of interest are in cases of interlocking boards of directors in industries that, on the surface, appear competitive. Let us first shed light on the term: Self-regulation refers to a normative order by a group! A group can be an industry association, a technology within an industry, hospitals operating under normative edicts of professional conduct, civil engineering, medical practices, and cultural affairs. This case addresses the technology of Artificial Intelligence, which is new and ubiquitous. The common denominator, in this case, is service. The term "service" includes both the creation of benefits for people and the prevention of harm. Underlying this line of thinking is the notion of giving more than taking. In an often-quoted speech, the 35th U.S. President Kennedy once said, "Ask not what your country can do for you,..." which phrase addressed the sentiment of service. It means that individually and collectively, ethical persons are to give more than taking and thereby create value.

Two organizations on which experience Artificial Intelligence advocates can build on, stand out. FINRA and ISO share an aspect of self-regulation. FINRA has the authority to write rules subject to approval from the Security and Exchange Commission (SEC) for the financial market. The International Organization for Standards (ISO) is an independent- and non-governmental organization devoted to quality standards for products and services. Artificial Intelligence is different from both FINRA and ISO in that it is a whole new technology and not a product or market.

Standards, values, and rules for exploring all Artificial Intelligence opportunities do not exist yet. Having ethical standards would contribute significantly to the harmony in trade and improvement of life- quality among people. A purely legislative approach to ethics comes with several negatives. Among those negatives are:

1. The time it takes to legislate and compromise between competing interest

2. The cost of compliance includes the penalties of non-compliance

3. The incompatibility of laws of different nations making compliance almost impossible for international firms

4. The inevitable costs being passed onto consumers

5. The need to enforce non-compliance across the globe

In comparison, a self-regulating ethical standard in Artificial Intelligence is

1. Much faster to establish standards

2. Does not impede legislation; in fact, it supports it

3. Creates future trust where none exists now.

Trust is an opportunity for value-creation by early-adopting corporations, as demonstrated by the experience of existing self-regulatory institutions described next.

The International Organization for Standards (ISO) is a Geneva-based independent, not-for-profit, non-governmental membership organization operating in 164 countries. The organization came into being in 1947. Of particular relevance to Artificial Intelligence are the ISO quality standards series 9000 for products and services, and 14000 on environmental issues, plus ISO - IEC 27001 on information security management services since 2008. Information security is one of many ethical issues as it focuses on preventing harm to people.

At ISO, *quality* for products and services is not a product specification as might be expected! Instead, quality is the quality of the processes that produce those products and services. The quality process is certified and re-certified after several years. The lesson for ethical standards in Artificial Intelligence is not defining ethics in specifics as "don't do this" but "do that." Ethics standards are best to evolve from practice and continually reviewed. A company's ISO certification creates trust in the market and considerable commercial value for its certified owner. Trust is a necessary ingredient for Artificial Intelligence as well. Similarly, the practice/process is relative to rights, conscience, wisdom, callings, obligations, limits and boundaries, control, and proofs from explained decisions will create trust and market value for those who practice it.

The Financial Industry Regulatory Authority (FINRA) protects investors by regulating their member broker-dealers, employees, and customers. FINRA, although authorized by the U.S. Congress, is not part of the U.S. government. It is a not-for-profit government corporation, and it is self-regulatory with rules subject to governmental approval by the Security and Exchange Commission (SEC). FINRA enforces securities broker-dealer's compliance with regulations of its own making but subject to government approval, settles industry disputes through mandatory arbitration and mediation, fosters market transparency, and promotes investor education. It has established a base of ethical rules in securities trading, observance of which is not optional. Ultimately, every investor receives a modicum of protection. For example, dealers of securities must be licensed, advertisements must be truthful and not misleading, investment products must be suitable, and complete information is required. FINRA membership, however, is not voluntary. A broker/agent's right to trade securities is a function of being qualified to do so and complying with the rules. The right to conduct business can be taken away after legal hearings.

The table below lists entities with a regulatory interest in Artificial Intelligence. It is not intended to be exhaustive but is descriptive. It shows who barks and who bites in these matters of regulating ethics.

Neither regulation nor self-regulation alone is a perfect remedy for all ethical dilemmas. In industry, Legislative codes adapt slowly to fast-changing markets, and the resulting time gap widens to resolve issues. Healthy self-regulation can only cover that portion of the market that is willing to comply. The rest have face litigation for their unethical practices and be named and shamed out of existence. The immediate goal is not one or the other but to start.

Table 3.1: *Summary of Selected Regulatory Forces*

A.I./ Ethics Regs	**Bark-Bite Scale 1.......50.......100**	**Influencer Force**	**Market Force**	**Europe Centric**	**The U.S. Centric**	**China Centric**
GDPR	x			x		
OECD	x	x		x	x	
White House	x	x			x	
State of California	x				x	
G 20	x	x		x	x	x
European Comm.	x	x		x		
UN/UNESCO	x	x		x	x	x
WTO	x	x		x	x	x
ITU	x		x	x	x	x
Self-Reg. model						
FINRA	x				x	
ISO	x		x	x	x	x

CHAPTER 4
THE CASE FOR STARTING WITH SELF-REGULATION FIRST

The time is Now!
The responsibility is ours!
Don't wait for miracles!

The path leading to ethics standards for this technology is thus far unclear. All the while, the technology is ubiquitous and is advancing fast. As this technology races head-first into an ethical vacuum, it creates an opportunity for technology leaders to entertain self-regulation to forestall impending difficulties. Enlightened self-interest, value creation, and trust should be sufficient motivation for a group of individual academics and business leaders to push for ethics standards. A good process starts with leading by example rather than preaching or grandstanding. Leading firms could voluntarily commit to clearly understood principles of conduct, where those principles are a lot more than the run of-the-mill mission statement. When sharing field-tested data, regulators can craft workable ethics rules to benefit the rest of us; as artificial intelligence becomes more embedded into the fabric of society, such private/public mechanisms can be a living foundation for constructive outcomes. The most apparent unethical outliers will become visible and subjected to public name and shame approaches or litigation under the laws. In the end, two new NGOs may dedicate themselves to their respective missions of supporting the positive and respectively protesting the negatives. Under this proposal, Artificial Intelligence and its related technologies have a chance to remain under human control.

Collective ethics governance starts with existing guidelines and gets refined by particular ethics cases bubbling up from industry experience. English common law is similar; it is a living structure. One can begin with a moral principle such as fairness and then adjudicate cases by what that means in industry X, applied to sector Y, in a given cultural setting Z. The critical point is that for ethical standards to evolve, both regulators and the regulated have to cooperate. The regulated and the regulators have to cooperate more and compete less. Pure competition produces winners and losers. The man-on-the-street must not always be the loser.

Approaches to Self-regulation in Artificial Intelligence

Formally, law is the rule by which everybody must live. But self-regulation has different meanings in different contexts. In explaining self-regulations, it may be illustrative to consider what self-regulation is not:

- Self-regulation is *no*t a call for all humans to arbitrarily constrain themselves in a particular way to meet a standard.
- Self-regulation is *not* about limiting a company's mission; a Mission statement typically addresses a given market, the company's contribution to that market, and how that company is different and often better than any other market participants.
- Self-regulation is *not* a suggestion for one sector in the economy to adopt identical ethics rules. For example, pharmaceuticals, civil engineering, direct marketing, and book publishing can have unique ethical practices within their sectors.
- Self-regulation is *not* compliance with external pressure groups.
- Self-regulation does *not* serve to stall formal regulation.
- Self-regulation is *not* laissez-faire capitalism, as opposed to central planning.

Self-regulation is a professional community's voluntary and normative order to accept standards and values that fit. The community, in this case, is made up of those who practice the technology of Artificial Intelligence. The ethic of that technology binds.

- Self-regulation *is* voluntary and privately self-enforcing. It will require a new organizational structure in the form of an NGO to become a business reality. Its governance will take the form of collaborative leadership.
- Self-regulation for Artificial Intelligence includes rulemaking and standards-setting for prescribed ethical conduct applicable to the technology, vendors, and clients.
- Self-regulation accepts and does not oppose a democratic government's legitimate quest for promulgating regulations for the common good.

Self-regulation has a spotty history in this technology and business in general. It has to overcome reasonable doubt before it becomes acceptable. In a positive example, efforts to voluntarily regulate regional fish harvesting for sustainability are clearly supportable. Efforts to self-regulate the aircraft industry failed badly when the US Federal Aviation Administration (FAA) certified Boeing's 747-MAX airliner as airworthy. The certification by former Boeing employees, then working for the FAA, was based on Boeings' reputation as a technology world leader. Two of those airliners crashed, and the rest is history. There are many lessons to be learned from that experience. This lesson is not to let the foxes guard the chicken coop.

A non-exhaustive summary of the pros and cons of self-regulation appears in the following tabulation:

Table 4.1

Strength	Weakness
Speed: in which ethics standards can be made operational	**Scam:** the public perception that self-regulation primarily serves industry
Flexibility: adjusting standards is more straightforward than passing new legislation	**Hide:** self-policing hides problems unknown to the public
Sensitivity: responding to the needs of the marketplace by people in the marketplace	**Appearance:** perception trumps problem-solving. Rumors outweigh good intentions.
Peer Pressure: to protect an industry's reputation and investments in the technology.	**Mixed results:** industry self-regulation has both failed and succeeded in the past.

Precedents for ethics standards in Artificial Intelligence

Around 1970, when the digital age more or less began, there arose a need to protect consumers from credit reporting abuse. The rule was that if you lose your card, all subsequent charges by thieves became the legal cardholders' responsibility. That rule's purpose was to protect the banks from default risk. It did not take long for regulators to establish the Fair Credit Reporting Act (FCRA) to protect consumers' privacy, fairness, and data accuracy. Once enacted, it reestablished trust in the field of credit finance.

As a consequence, the industry flourished. In 1974, the government stepped in again to pass the Fair Credit Billing Act (FCBA) to protect consumers from unfair billing practices such as unauthorized transactions, undelivered goods, and more. That Act, too, resulted in new trust and the credit card business flourished even more.

What do these two situations have in common? (a) an injustice happened, and the law stepped in to correct it proactively, (b) the results were the restoration of fairness and economic growth, and both consumers and vendors were happy. This time, for artificial intelligence, the situation is a little different. We are dealing with a ubiquitous technology applied to all levels in society. There are two reasons why blithely repeating past approaches is not reasonable. Credit, banking, and consumer finance rules apply to an industrial sector. On the other hand, Artificial Intelligence is not that well understood, is not an industrial sector, and not an industry. Artificial Intelligence is a force, and it cannot be banned. So, now what?

What is needed now is an initiative to engage many voices :

> For the private sector the job is to formulate domain-specific business ethics standards is principally to protect the public, protect corporate reputations, and encourage economic growth. For NGO organizations with deep domain knowledge the job is to lead the charge for ethical standards.
>
> Lawmakers drafting precision legislation should address facial recognition, biometrics, and dual military/civil society technologies.

The term *precision legislation* means writing rules that link to existing laws. Take the example of precision legislation in the Advancing Precision Medicine Act (2016). It encourages the US Department of Health and Human Services with new initiatives to prevent, diagnose, and treat diseases. Similarly, lawmakers resort to precision legislation to address biometric or surveillance technologies to protect people. *Precision legislation,* therefore, is the mechanism under which laws adjust to new conditions that lawmakers could not possibly have foreseen a short time ago. With NGOs experimenting with Artificial Intelligence ethics standards in a market, lawmakers will be able to write precision legislation faster and better for the benefit of people and keep a human lid on the technology.

Cultures around the world differ widely, and judging them is not the issue here. Human cultures evolve from climate, food options, beliefs, habits, and language. *Vive la difference*! In the Near and Far East, a person has reached adulthood once married. The institution of marriage is to have children. Locally, people become adults around age 18 and generally get married because of love and desire for children. Culture dictates how one must deal with equality and rights, and culture trumps technology. The western world, composed of the European Union, North- and most of South America, and the remaining English-speaking world, is somewhat different. The United States is considered exceptional and the product of its relatively short history:

- The US Constitution partly enshrines the American dream. The issues are rights and opportunities for all citizens and the expectation that individuals reach their highest ambitions based on effort. Technology, therefore, must not impede these ideals. The American Dream is an entitlement for individual rights, not a personal right to own stuff.

- The rights of equality, liberty, and brotherhood come from the French Revolution and are American values. Equality refers to non-discrimination, among others. A US ethical standard may never permit Artificial Intelligence apps to compromise an individual's equality before the law. Equality, on the other hand, does not also mean that all persons are identical. The uniqueness of the individual is an essential consideration. Artificial Intelligence technology also lends itself to segregating people by targets, rich from poor, and endless varieties of groups A from groups B, which could quickly become the vehicle for unconstitutional inequality.

- Historically, the culture of American Exceptionalism means pragmatism, which is a *can-do* attitude among the general population. This attitude became necessary shortly after The Mayflower landed on Plymouth Rock in 1620, and it was the survival response to the obstacles early settlers had to overcome. It was not an ideology they brought with them from Anglican England; instead, it was a value system they created themselves, and the rest of us more or less grew up with it. The Pilgrim culture means separatism, which at the time was a rebellion against the Church of England. Today, North American culture embraces informality. North American informality manifests itself in fewer bureaucratic obstacles and high value for individual initiatives. It is not uncommon for garage projects to turn into unicorns. A unicorn is understood to be a start-up enterprise with more than $1 billion in revenue. A historical example of exceptionalism is the Wright brothers' contribution to aviation, their determination, their innovative engineering in the wing design to induce lift, experimenting with wind tunnels, and above all, risking their resources and lives for the cause of flying. Similar values are possible to emerge from Artificial Intelligence. Airplanes have crashed in the past, and many autonomous taxis in the future will have accidents as well. The goal is not to avoid all negatives. The goal is for the ratio of positives to be more significant.

- Freedom of speech is enshrined in American law and is highly valued and defended by people. The technology of Artificial Intelligence lends itself to its suppression and manipulation. Media abuses of free speech become an issue at each election cycle, and their methodologies and effects on election results raise the peoples' excitement.

What we are seeking to achieve by Artificial Intelligence self-regulation is a good life for all people! A good life does not define the purpose of life, nor does it explain the meaning of life. Good experiences resulting from technology assure safety, protect properties, provide security of the persons, healthy habitats with food security, and general abundance and well-being. Utilitarianism philosophy fits the bill.

What we have now, or the state this technology is in, is not anywhere near what we seek for ourselves. We have to find and implement ethics standards for the technology of Artificial Intelligence. The business metaphor is that "if we do not know where we intend to go, we wind- up elsewhere." Even if we know a path to implement good ethics, there is no guarantee that we will get there as those principles still have to be made operational and thus accepted by most.

Have good attitudes

Moral standards for Artificial Intelligence are unlikely to appear by themselves. To eventually have ethical standards in practice requires an operating apparatus to make that happen. Such an operation must lead industries towards continually higher levels of ethics in Artificial Intelligence. In practice, that means an improving level of harmony among consumers and producers and with fewer injustices along the way. Two separate and distinct not-for-profit organizations can achieve that; one for willing producers to accept self-constraints and another for the unwilling to be shamed into it, or by litigation if all fails. For establishing moral responsibility, one should start with two questions and place them side by side. These questions are *what should happen, and what could happen,* in this technology? Add to that a reality check that not all initially good intentions produce good outcomes. Even with plenty of hype and structural uncertainty, the expectation is that vastly more benefit than detriment will come from Artificial Intelligence undertakings. A lot depends on answers to the question of what could and should occur from now on?

Under conventional presumptions, developers have care-ethics responsibility for all their innovations. Care ethics applies to the producers and includes companies that install this technology, investors who finance such projects. Fair accountability also means consumers transparency in clear language. Fantastic predictions for technological benefits must be plausible and predicting disasters realistic as well. "Buyers Beware" is an accepted standard in commerce, and it applies to ethics.

Among the many responsibilities of operations management is compliance with regulations. That is so whether mandated by law or also voluntary subscribed to, as suggested in this book. The operations department in companies is the source of most administrative data. Productivity improvements (output/input) have continued to be goals since the mid-last century. Increased operations complexity requires more steps and, with it, more paper, while digitization reduces paper. The net effect is minor for the paper-reduction but significant for data and information. The market requires near-instant and accurate information on customers, contract provisions, and due dates approaching in real-time. Regulatory technology is known as TechReg. It includes cybersecurity needed in opposing unethical conduct in Artificial Intelligence. Ironically, this technology incorporates ethically controversial surveillance technologies helpful in causing and preventing undesirable effects. Cybersecurity and surveillance management depend on massive amounts of data in digital-, image-, speech-, and voice formats. Corporate use is both defensive and offensive when applied globally and domestically.

In biblical times the pronunciation of the word *shibboleth* was enough to identify a friend or a foe. In modern times surveillance technology words still matter. The technology uses lexicon-based deciphering for tone and sentiment, plus code-words. Companies surveil communications between workers and customers across all channels like e-mail, social media, and text. Understandably, many corporate risks originate from the inside and the outside, against which a corporation must defend. The world described by George Orwell in the book *Nineteen Eighty-Four* is fast approaching. Internal ethical lapses are insider trading, tax evasion, bribery, financing terrorism, and money laundering, to name a few. Outsider ethical lapses relate to former employee-employer issues enabled by regulated bounties such as whistleblowing. The technology serves Artificial Intelligence on the one hand, and deters on the other hand. Both good guys vs. bad ones have access to the same Artificial Intelligence.

Attitudes that mislead and may cause ethical compromises

Over- and underestimating AI 'projects'. The impacts of new technologies are traditionally overestimated in the short run and underestimated in the long run. This pattern has been evident in wind power, solar power, and genome sequencing. In Artificial Intelligence, the public is initially told of revolutionary promises, only to find big disappointments in the short term. Gartner, a research firm, publishes what they call a "hype cycle"; it documents hype graphically for many industries, even by different applications within Artificial Intelligence.

Artificial Intelligence is magic. This technology is presumed to produce magical results, solely evidenced by supposed industry experts in front of microphones. Sages and champions do occasionally err. For instance, Long Term Capital, a hedge fund managed by Nobel Laureates Scholes and Merton, became nearly insolvent on excessive leverage in 1998, losing $500m in one day, requiring a $3.6b bank bail-out. The lesson is that even gurus are subject to emotions and believe what they think.

Drawing general conclusions from a single favorable result. The illogic goes like this: (a) make an observation suggesting a cause-effect relationship exists, (b) believe that this is probably true, (c) because you think it is probably true, you are nearly sure that it is true, (d) and then act on your belief. Ethically, relying on the rules of evidence is better. Under US law, those rules require relevance, materiality, and competence.

Nearly every technology develops an insider *jargon*. Jargons may help introduce new technology and also serve to obfuscate and promote self-importance. Take machine learning, ML, for short. Is it true that machines act like humans after acquiring knowledge? Of course not. They can narrowly mimic humans, with warts and all, an expression attributed to Lord Cromwell (1599 – 1658). The problem is that the word "learning" can relate to many different experiences. Technology promoters use the term loosely, and readers rarely question it, resulting in misunderstandings.

Exponential-ism. The adjective "exponential" is a hype term in Artificial Intelligence. A statement like "facial recognition technologies are growing exponentially worldwide" is an example of that. What the authors mean is "rapid" rather than "exponential." For something to be exponential, somebody must have an exponent in mind.

Artificial Intelligence will take over the world. Its algorithms and self-aware machines may eventually become malevolent and dominate us all, leading to an apocalypse, the end of the world as we imagine it. Vivid imaginations can be both constructive and entertaining. However, one should take such scenarios with a grain of salt. There is no evidence that humans can create something bigger than themselves, notwithstanding Ray Kurzweil (US futurist). Louis XVI (1754 – 1774) took the attitude of *"apres nous, le deluge."*

Attitudes that may lead to change

Purpose comes before motivation and must be well articulated. For example, ask whether a project could be motivated by undesirable ends? If so, find out from whose perspective? If one party's gain equals another party's loss, it is a zero-sum game; ethically, this may not be good enough. A monopoly may be desirable from the monopolist's point of view, but it is undesirable from all others, and it may not even be illegal in all instances. For example, a business strategy called *copy, acquire and kill* emerged from 2020 Congressional hearings on five large firms' dominant position. Under that scheme, when a competitor appears, the market leader will copy that approach and unsuccessfully perhaps compete, acquire the small firm at a premium to the most agreeable principals, and kill its technology. This method is not illegal, and nobody even gets visibly hurt. It is lucrative because the now rich former competitors got paid, a competitive headache is solved, and nobody got hurt, except perhaps society in the long run.

Intelligence as a technology lacks contextual awareness. Intelligence rarely focuses on only one target. A military robot may not distinguish between an enemy in uniform and a civilian. That may cause what is called collateral damage. Or police chiefs may become over-confident in their technological capability and decide to close the option of a non-force conflict resolution. Substituting the term "police commander" with "corporate CEO" is ethically similar. If a project intends to innovate for increases in productivity, greener products, protection of endangered species, customer service, and a higher standard of living, it is ethically well positioned.

Confidence is what can emerge from organizational preparedness for technological change. Firms need physically and culturally prepare for the new digital frontier. A digital transformation should be ongoing for workers, suppliers, customers, stakeholders, and consumers in which each party understands the evolving business model and embraces a new culture. In most companies, this preparedness is certifiably still absent. Overconfidence may lead to spectacular crashes, and under-confidence can lead to lost opportunities. Management must thus balance reality with hope. That, in turn, differs from case to case. The balancing act includes continuous education at all levels.

Accountability means presenting a correct narrative, among which are matters like liability, promises, and more. Lack of this responsibility occurs when an intelligent agent acts independently and concurrently with humans who are responsible. Needed are case-specific rules to guide peoples' choices and machine choices. When an intelligent agent diagnoses a patients' ailment, what is the doctors' accountability for either (a) ignoring it or (b) following it (c) or the machine agent misleading the doctor? Sophia is a robot in Saudi Arabia declared a "citizen" of that country with perhaps a more generous free speech right than its natural citizens have. To whom is Sophia ethically accountable? Corporations are legally defined as "persons" with First Amendment rights under the Constitution in the US. Legal experts in the UK contemplate personhood for robots to deal with liability issues arising in the marketplace.

Jobs, jobs, and more jobs: Throughout industrial history, successive waves of automation have created more jobs than were eliminated, although neither at the same skill level nor at the same time. Can one expect a repeat performance for the technology of Artificial Intelligence? The Spinning Jenny (1770+) made it possible to create clothes from more than one spindle at a time. Ford's automobile assembly line (1920+) made it possible for citizens to have cars and have middle-class jobs. In each case, the need for employment grew. The new technologies we are facing now are different in many respects; for one, new technologies are likely to replace many middle-class jobs. The new job category is the digital worker.

Those jobs require coding skills and talents that were not needed a few decades ago. An employment gap is developing and an income gap with it. Some people will labor full time, and others only are on a part-time or contract. In fact, in an upside-down world of Artificial Intelligence, it may turn out that society's upper strata go to work, while the lower one is on government-guaranteed minimum income.

While material, labor, and capital costs are elements of any commercial project, for Artificial Intelligence, different variables have to be considered. Machine learning requires a considerable number of low-cost workers to label images and interpret words. That holds until such a time when machines use synthetic data, as in facial recognition applications. Ethically, the mid -20th Century data processing phenom called Garbage-in/Garbage-out (GIGO) may have to be revisited soon concerning synthetic data machine learning. Similarly, inappropriate speech needs to be filtered out of social media, requiring many employees to do the initial work of data tagging. Workers cannot perform that function until the definition of "inappropriate speech" is defined. The downside is that those jobs are likely gone soon, and those skills have no enduring value, to begin with. The ethics issue comes from creating a few million jobs and their eradication a short time later. People are not inanimate things!

Risk is part of business life. A good understanding of failure risks in many dimensions is a minimum requirement of managers. For a project in Artificial Intelligence technologies, there are unique considerations. Some advanced applications employ vision technologies to perceive objects, followed by language technology to describe an object's image. Combining two or more technologies in one application is extraordinarily complex and can easily reach logical- and computational limits to remain reliable. The same principle works in other fields as well. An airline pilot may deal with one malfunction at a time, but two or more simultaneous malfunctions in the air become very dangerous.

CHAPTER 5
WHAT TO REGULATE, THAT IS THE ETHICS QUESTION

Recalling the goal, it is for humans to remain in absolute control of the Artificial Intelligence technology. That is for the sake of not losing control by default, on which occasion the opportunists of the world have a field day. That is a real possibility and ultimate disaster. "Never, never, ever to give up" on this is the Churchillian answer to the plausibility of this technology winding up in self-serving hands, and we, the humans, marching towards selfdom, to borrow language from Friedrich Hayek. Conversely, it is also not intended to suggest that new ethics for Artificial Intelligence standards consider every concept covered in this chapter. The following fourteen concepts are ideas for consideration before charging ahead.

"What" to regulate is only one part of the question; the others are the "Why and the How" of self-constraint is the other part of the same question. If a concept has survived thousands of years, it is time to take it seriously. In that spirit, a look at the classics is warranted.

This chapter explores well-known ethics concepts and links those to Artificial Intelligence, the technology. The main concern is not to debate the merit of a philosophy. We start with the presumption that corporate leaders do not spend all their time on ingenious methods to exploit their customers unethically. Some do, but there are ways to handle those as well. Ethical standards in Artificial Intelligence will have to allow for cultural differences to flourish. Rather than aiming for one size to fit all, one can just as quickly admire differences. Ethics concepts under consideration are conscience, rights, wisdom, callings, obligation, limits, fairness, full disclosure, monopoly, and beneficence. The discussion that follows comes from a Western Judeo/Christian history perspective. Finally, many ethics cases are industry-specific and need to evolve from the ground up.

Conscience

The term conscience refers to the perception of what may be right or wrong with Artificial Intelligence models, algorithms, or objects. In other words, what happens before, during, and after an algorithm has been deployed? Is a models' outcome contrary to moral standards and values we hold? The similar-sounding term "conscientious" only suggests that an algorithm is the best possible. It is a goal that a machine learning algorithm *in good conscience* does not violate ethics and *has humans* monitor it. Science fiction writers talk a lot about robots with self-awareness, having consciousness, cognition, and a mind of their own. For the time being, this remains fiction without science, and probably for a long time after that.

The simplest way to define the meaning of the word *conscience* is to separate what is right from what is wrong. Alternatively, to separate what works from that which does not work, If a model works without harming, it is good. If a model does not work for any remaining reason and harms, it has to be stopped. Even if a model does both harm and good, it has to be stopped and at least evaluated. As a practical matter, machine learning applications in healthcare raise different moral implications than a machine learning application for autonomous vehicles. It is evident that ethics segmentation by the industry sector is a necessity. Moral values for conscience in healthcare, finance, law enforcement, or consumer marketing are different. In healthcare, morality is a function of the number of people being helped v the number hurt. In finance, one weighs morality in terms of protection v exploitation. In law enforcement, dual technologies serve both to prevent- crime and commit a crime; in marketing, society has to deal with unwanted targeting of individuals by commerce.

In medical markets, the intelligent processing of millions of records per day creates value for the industry and its customers without raising too many questions. A conscience-related question may relate to what purpose data serves and its accuracy, security, and institutional needs. Unconscionable applications in the $3.6+ T US healthcare market most often involve money issues in the form of price-fixing in medical supplies and a resulting concentration of economic power. That is a matter of law enforcement as well as ethics.

In clinical medicine, the matter of conscience is even more apropos. Take medical imaging, for example. Neural networks have learned to identify skin cancer nearly as well as have dermatologists. The algorithms examine the image of a melanoma's size, color, depth, and edge patterns to conclude the look-see with a decision. That is ethically good as it is cheap and for patients. One risk side are doctors who may become overly reliant on those models: ditto for prescriptions! Generally, it is ethically sound when 96 people out of 100 benefit and four do not. But when four people out of one hundred suffer because of neglectful over-reliance on algorithms, it requires another look. The American Cancer Society estimates melanoma diagnoses for 2020 to exceed 100,000 cases with 6,800 fatalities. A fundamental rule in Artificial Intelligence is never to leave machines and models in an unsupervised execution.

Diagnoses of medical conditions are not the only Artificial Intelligence applications where conscience is a consideration. Neural networks can also help identify plausible causes of human ailments. Machine deep learning algorithms search for hidden patterns in Big Data. Big Data means enormous data sets in many formats such as print, digital, and image to find hidden correlations. To do this may require super-computers, such as IBM's Watson or quantum computing just around the corner. Ethically there is nothing wrong, except that finding correlations is not the same as identifying causes. Again, an ethical problem does not emerge from the technology itself. It appears from its interpretation by and among people, some with bad attitudes like excessive competition. Every graduate student with access to statistical software can run correlation analyses and get results. In the popular literature, such findings state it "supports" something, "helps" with a condition, may even help "prevent". For studies to be considered scientific, other researchers doing a remarkably similar investigation would have to come up with similar results.

In the finance sector, the core objective is to make money, which most people accept as moral. The "how and what for" question may raise ethical concerns, however. In our society, inequality raises public concerns. Anybody who makes a lot more and physically does not work as hard must be unethical. Theft, tax evasion, and extortion are ethically wrong. The remedies for these are in the law. The moral good in high-speed trading is that it provides market liquidity, which means that if a person needs to sell, there is a customer to buy on the other end. That is a moral good because it serves a human. Broker-Dealers with faster computers and more PhDs in their workforce may also be more profitable than those with slower computers and fewer PhDs. Fair enough! That is competition, and it is also considered acceptable in democratic nations.

Conscience issues can also arise from (a) Spoofing, a method to enter market orders without executing them to fake demand that leads to a rise in price. It can also arise from (b) Quote stuffing, flooding the market with orders, causing response delays to induce arbitrage opportunities. Who may benefit? Presumably, those broker-dealers invested in the most skilled workers and the fastest computers acting in split seconds. Who gets hurt? Probably nobody directly. Thus, spoofing and quote stuffing is both theoretically legal and only moderately unethical, and on top of that, very profitable? The technology of Artificial Intelligence need not be the cause. What is next in the technological progression, and would management with a conscience engage in these activities, whether it qualifies as Artificial Intelligence or not?

A regulatory and even self-regulatory watchful agent has to be in place to avoid runaway or near abuse. That agent has to be human, but can be assisted by digital ethics agents as well.

Rights

Rights refer to the natural person; the Right to work, own property, happiness, and fellowship are all rights. One defining document for such rights is the U.S. Constitution's Bill of Rights, the United Nations' Declaration of Human Rights, and the Geneva Convention for the conduct of war. The emerging technologies of Artificial Intelligence must not violate rights, intentionally or accidentally.

So much for the basics! Human Rights has an extensive body of literature, and Artificial Intelligence lends itself well to deprive humans of those rights in new ways. In this chapter, the goal is to find guidance for behaving ethically in managing this technology. The emphasis is on the utilitarian rights of maximizing good outcomes and minimizing harmful effects, recognizing that perfection is hard to achieve and define. Good results pertain to life and liberty, while negative outcome rights refer to not harming natural persons. Under ideal circumstances, one imagines a corporate board addressing questions like these before approving a business plan using artificial intelligence. Questioning why we are doing this, who benefits plus who gets hurt, whether this project ever ends, and so on, has to occur. Boards are the ones to ask questions because they have the means of stopping risky ventures. In March 2018, the Toronto Declaration, sponsored by Amnesty International and related partner organizations, was released. It addresses the decision-making problems caused by opaque and unexplained machine learning. An ethical concern is that what machines learn from the past, they are condemned to repeat. Back in 1948, the United Nations General Assembly passed the Universal Declaration of Human Rights. Among its list of 30 Rights touching on this technology are the following:

Equality

The lead agency for Artificial Intelligence at the United Nations is the ITU working under the motto *A.I. for Good*. Equality aims to narrow the digital divide among the world's people, access to health services, and sustainable cities.

Discrimination

Redlining is a process of charging higher interest rates for people in more impoverished neighborhoods based on perceived risk factors. The experience with microlending has rendered the perception of the increased risk of poor people to be false. The community, and not the personal attributes of a member of that community, define all members. Machines learn from historical data and, therefore, are presumed to repeat biases embedded in the data. In defense of machines, they are not immoral. People who accept machine results without questioning are undoubtedly guilty of negligence.

Arbitrary Arrests

The technology of face recognition greatly aids the dictators of the world in suppressing their political opponents.

Freedom of Opinion

Consider what is involved in fake news, which thrives on misleading information from discredited sources. The enabling technology comprises website publishing, media technology, and algorithms that feed on human gullibility.

The Right to Desirable Work

The term "desirable" means the Right to work, free choice of employment, and unemployment protection. It does not mean a good job; it only implies a willingness to work. In evaluating existing- and future projects, an employment opportunity is considered an ethics mandate.

Freedom from State interference of rights

Large data sets, fast computing, together with do empower some governments, especially non-democratic ones, to stifle dissent. Examples are withholding unfavorable news, disabling critical news sources, and massive invasion into the private lives of millions of people hooked on free services.

The Right to be Forgotten v the wish to be remembered

This idea is a product of the time we live in. One would think that when humans spend so much effort on elaborate cemetery tombs, listing titles, honors, and creating heirlooms to be remembered, that the Right to be forgotten would never come up. But here it is. In the E.U. and Argentina since 2016, the forgotten option is a legally enforceable right. Technically it is a right to have specific personal data erased from searchable databases. It protects people with now settled previous legal entanglements to live free. Thankfully, there is no corresponding right to be remembered.

A calling

The calling is what we humans are *made* for. It differs from a corporate mission statement in what we are *paid* for.

The meaning of a calling is to contribute to an improved way of life. It always refers to something constructive and is often based on faith or ethical values like compassion and respect. "Ethics" has its roots in Greek, meaning "of moral character."

In the corporate world, where a company is indeed a person, a calling is their *raison d'etre*. It explains the reason for their existence. Many are more show than substance. The mission statement clarifies for public consumption who we are, what we do, and why we do it while implying we are doing it better than everybody else. The vision statement identifies a particular view of the near future into which the mission fits. These statements generally take a position on governance, management policies, and fiduciary responsibility, and social duties regarding virtue, commitment, and outcomes affecting clients and society in general. The common belief is that without ethics, a corporation cannot survive and grow. At the same time, with ethics, a corporations' survival is not guaranteed either.

Some examples of companies and institutions' vision and mission statements align with Artificial Intelligence and their relevance for regulatory considerations. The mission and vision statements quite often tend to be a bit pompous. Paraphrasing from selected entities:

> AMAZON is concentrating on providing services for worldwide *customers to find everything.* The personal, corporate values hint at the pursuit of monopoly in that it covers the entire world for every existing product. Monopoly is legally defined case by case, and the ethical rules of economic ambition remain somewhat vague. In each case, the company remains innocent until proven otherwise.
>
> GOOGLE promises *to organize the world's information* and make it accessible and useful. The company intended to take on the whole world, and the term "useful" omits useful for whom and what purpose, good or evil? The company also crafted its corporate motto, "to do no evil." This statement means that Google has at least considered that possibility, understands the potential for doing evil, and has decided not to do so. (at this time). Being aware that evil is always possible and conscientiously not becoming evil is at least commendably honest. A future Google Board may act in anger at regulators for restricting their power and limiting their income. Influential enterprises may find themselves on the defensive for no other reason than being influential.
>
> APPLE *lives on planet Earth to produce excellent products and great new experiences* for customers. It accomplishes that with hardware, software, and services for phones and computers. Personal, corporate values and public ones are not in conflict, per se. From the regulatory point of view, that by itself need not alarm anybody. With a quarter of a trillion dollars in annual revenue, Apple too has to defend its success.

> TESLA wants *to accelerate the transition to sustainability* in energy, according to its mission and vision statements. That is pure goodness and would even please the United Nations with Sustainable Development. Sustainability means more than just keeping going. In 1987 the United Nations commissioned Brundtland, a former Norwegian prime minister, to examine sustainability. The Commission bearing his name defined sustainability as follows: "meeting the needs of the present generation without compromising future generations to meet their own needs." The report is in a book called "Our Common Future." The ethical obligation of stewardship for the next generations is often, and conveniently, overlooked in businesses overwhelmed with short-term survival.

Tesla's vision statement includes commitments not to cut corners, not settle for compromises, and not accept anything less than perfect. Those values apply to all three of Tesla's industrial segments of electric cars, solar energy, and Space-X, aiming to reach Mars within our lifetime. Broadly defined, public and private values align. The ethical issues Tesla raises differ from those of other companies in that they are more far-reaching.

OPEN AI is a research and deployment company with a mission to assure safety and social benefit in "AI". Tesla and OpenAI share the founding *principles and principal*, Elon Musk, and both recognize the magnitude of unresolved ethical issues. It is a constructive approach to upcoming cooperation between the private- and public sectors. OpenAI is also the developer and owner of GPT-3, a learning algorithm that can draft poems and text good enough to fool the average human reader. Reaching back into Artificial Intelligence archives, one has to realize that machine intelligence was defined by Turing (1912 – 1954), particularly by the Turing Test. The test finds that if a machine's response is indistinguishable from a human one to the same question, then machine intelligence is present.

The not-for-profit sector almost always addresses moral causes, and therefore it falls outside of this purview. The U.S. Red Cross exists to prevent suffering. The Rockefeller Foundation is about humanity's well-being, and Harvard University Business School is about training the next generation of leaders and setting standards in education.

For corporations, the operating priorities have to align with the ethics of its calling.

Obligation

Having an obligation refers to a requirement to either do something or refrain from doing something else because we "owe." For example, we owe our aging parents respect and support because they cared for us. Caring may require reciprocity, and it applies to countless other instances. That parental caring obligation is a moral one and, in some countries, a legal one. In Germany, grown children have a legal obligation to contribute to the cost of their aging- and needy parents. But ethical obligations are not the same as legal ones, especially when it comes to Artificial Intelligence. When something goes wrong, compliance with the law is not the same as compliance with a moral standard. Moral standards apply to employment shifts, liability compensation, trust in the technology, consequential human economic inequality that may weaken the middle class, undermine democratic institutions, to fairness, and to truth-telling in commerce, to name a few.

We do not have any workable moral standards for Artificial Intelligence yet. Defining ethical standards is extremely hard to do if a buy-in by people is also needed. In the past, religions led the way towards morality as they viewed them. Geographically, human history, language, and climate influence morality as well. However, we are comfortable with common sense judgments based on shared everyday experiences. In a democracy with social capitalism, peaceful adjustments are possible to accommodate changing times. However, under emerging Artificial Intelligence technology, we may have to say farewell to common- sense. That is a dangerous point to find ourselves at. The following paragraph on "wisdom" may help the reader think about our near tech future. That calls for wisdom.

Wisdom

Let the real subject experts in our communities that is, corporate management, software developers, financiers, customers, regulators, jointly ask themselves the following questions:

Is this new widget I am doing legal?

Is this moral, from development, to use, and to retirement?

Does Artificial Intelligence solve the problem or do something else, like hiding it?

Are the metrics appropriate, and who will maintain what I am doing after I have moved on?

What is the actual impact – primary, secondary, and tertiary?

Is the worst-case scenario plausible?

Most business leaders are presumed to have sufficient work experience and subject knowledge to practice good judgment. To be generous, let us also assume that most business leaders do not spend all their time finding ways to exploit their customers or kill competitors. However, business leaders are also human beings and, therefore, not infallible. A well-known figure- of- speech states that "power corrupts, and absolute power corrupts absolutely (Lord Acton, 1887). No person and no enterprise stays still and remains as perhaps idealistic in the end as they were in the beginning.

To understand the meaning of wisdom with Artificial Intelligence, a consultation with a wisdom source, namely Socrates (470-399), is called for. He advised first to reflect on what it means to be human, and secondly, to engage in what it takes to live an extraordinary life. Exploring this question leads to thinking about the unknown. That unknown may very well relate to wisdom. Whoever displays a modicum of humility may be presumed to have wisdom.

The idea of avoiding harm has its origin in the Hippocratic oath as applied in medicine. Superficially, an enterprise may convince itself that by not harming customers, it does good. For example, natural language processing helps communications in international trade, and facial recognition serves security; robots assist humans and have not yet turned against us. General automation helps reduce cost and eliminates waste. So, what is the problem?

To not harm is simply not enough! The word "intelligence" on A.I. is often, and mistakenly, considered as clever, resulting in an advantage over a competitor. That also is not enough! Under ideal circumstances, the technology must align with the noble values expressed in the mission- and vision statement. The wisdom in Artificial Intelligence wisdom must help a corporation flourish in the long term. Corporate flourishing includes workers, customers, investors, and the communities in which the corporation operates. If the clients are global, then ethically, our planet is the corporate oyster.

Limits and Boundaries

The word "limit" suggests that there are ceilings that this technology must meet when dealing with humans. The word "boundaries" refers to the relationship between humans themselves as a result of the technologies. Having care and value means respect for human values, as mentioned earlier. Human values can be embedded into a robots' logic and into algorithms to assure ethical outcomes. But the question is, whose human value? In our international world, that becomes culture-specific and different for East/West or North/South. The "value" of a pending automated decision depends on the degree of importance to the sponsoring entity. Automation project evaluations must account for integrity, honesty, promises, and trust, among others, from project start to project end. The absolute control of any Artificial Intelligence application must always be linked to a human being to assure control, safety, social well-being.

Ethical relationships between doctors and patients, between lawyers and clients, and between regulators and the regulated, are reasonably well developed and understood and most of the time practiced. When it comes to Artificial Intelligence, the relationship is between the provider and the technology user. At a minimum, accountability is best by case law, or even better, by mediated self-regulation. For example, suppose massive destruction of employment opportunities arises from Artificial Intelligence induced automation schemes. In that case, government and the private sectors have to step in early to prevent social disasters.

Fairness and Equity

Fairness and equity are value-laden terms. Equity is a quality of being impartial. A critical question is to what extent does this technology hinder or enable citizens to perceive and ameliorate imbalances correctly? Since fairness in absolute terms is difficult to define, much less to achieve, self-regulation has a prominent role in alternative dispute resolutions. The core technologies of machine learning, neural networks, and robotics are by themselves value-neutral. How these technologies are applied is what matters. If used unfairly, then a correction must be available in the future.

Technology can serve good and evil equally well. How people use it is somewhat controllable but not completely stoppable.

Suppose racism, unfairness, is a prejudice and discrimination *against* a class of human beings in a numerical minority. In that case, it is required to apply this technology to prevent harm to humans. Containing racism itself, however, may be a matter of another discipline, like education, for instance. If inequality is defined as a lack of opportunity to achieve equality caused mainly through Artificial Intelligence, then moral liability is present once proved. The remedies lie with regulators and practitioners.

Fairness is an ethical mandate, while achieving absolute equality in everything is neither possible nor is it even designable. When facial recognition errs, some false arrests can happen; and in some nations, arrested persons may even have to prove their innocence before being released. When autonomous systems do not recognize a population class because of under-representation in training data, serious injuries may result. A malicious intent need not be the reason for a bad outcome. It is more likely to happen when human controls fail.

Similarly, a lack of critical forethought at a project's inception stage is another cause. Both insufficient data and mislabeling may lead to misidentification. Given a search category of "cute baby face," the result will be determined by what some distant analyst/labeler decided "cute" means. Also, in algorithms trained on felony cases to construct profiles for early prisoner release recommendations, the machine may indeed err, as in nearly any other technology introduction.

Beneficence

Who would have thought that ideas like altruism, merci, generosity have a role in commerce today, particularly in Artificial Intelligence? They do and always did.

Historically, beneficence arrived with the works of David Hume (1711-1776), J. S. Mills (1806-1873), and Emanuel Kant (1774-1804). Hume's writings are about virtue ethics, which he calls beneficence. Apart from benevolence, he accepts human nature as subject to egoists and points out that we all have fears, ambitions, and an existential need for survival. As already mentioned, J.S. Mills came up with the philosophy of Utilitarianism as the pursuit of the greatest happiness. Utilitarianism is also welfare-oriented, as what is right is also good. Kant, being German, defined many maxims in terms of duty.

Duty surprisingly includes the obligation, not the option, of beneficence. According to Kant, everybody must practice beneficence limited only by individual comfort zones and in a total absence of implied gain. Global corporate chieftains should note that making charitable contributions to their best clients' favorite humanitarian cause would not cut muster with Emanuel.

Translating this historical precedent into 21st Century guidance for business standards is not all that straightforward. It raises many questions like these:

> Does ethical Artificial Intelligence have an obligation to be beneficent?
>
> Is beneficence a moral ideal for which to strive! Can it therefore be regulated?

Some aspects of philosophical beneficence are already in everyday use. The U.S. Coast Guard rescues sinking ships at sea; we help a disabled person across the street, for example. It gets fuzzy when determining how much money a wealthy person should donate to charity to be morally beneficent? Some of our acts of beneficence may involve reducing small children's choices to avoid injury.

But how about accepting involuntary payroll deductions to cover employer-mandated life insurance you do not need or a labor union membership fee for a union you do not belong to. The unintended price of beneficence, in some instances, is having fewer choices. In western democracies, personal autonomy is valued and a right. Conversely, in socialist nations, lower personal independence is more acceptable and justified by the common good. Artificial Intelligence lends itself to both greater freedom and less freedom.

In the biomedical field, beneficence is an issue in the Belmont Report (National Commission of Human Subjects 1978). The National Commission wrote it for the Protection of Human subject of behavioral and biomedical research.

A historical reference comes from Adam Smith's (1723-1790) classic book The Wealth of Nations. Here, the practice of self-interest regarding land, labor, and capital delivers good things for all people, which to a casual observer sounds counter-intuitive. Smith's capitalist benevolence is an "invisible hand" providing all that is good.

Unintended outcomes

The category of unintended outcomes is a considerable risk in Artificial Intelligence and often results from lack of oversight. Self-regulation, self-discipline to weed out bad science is a more realistic approach to address that problem. Unintended consequences can also be positive if, for example, an existing pharmaceutical product coincidentally also leads to curing an entirely different disease.

In the short term, there are some lousy science examples in this category. Systems to predict low recidivism for early release of convicts from prisons rely on unreliable criminal profiles. A false positive can be fatal. A massive resume machine reading program for a corporate recruitment program turned out to be biased towards males because the training data was ten years old. Nearly half of all Dow Jones stock market trades are machine-generated, causing unintended volatility when all algorithms decide to sell on the same signal. The people who wrote the software, also known as "quants," read and publish in the same journals. Nefarious logic programmed into computer models may subtly support racial profiling without being detected.

Recommendation models derived from personal profiles tell us what to read, what movie to see, and what products to buy. It is more than coincidental that the recommenders often happen to sell those products. The long-term unintended result is a potential cultural change limiting human exploration and discovery. It used to be a rule by which people can influence others, and now algorithms do that on behalf of the managerial class. Mechanizing human choices can also lead to the elimination of empathy in customer service. A human touch story came when an L.L. Bean telephone operator took the initiative to personally deliver a sailboat to a customer after recognizing that the company had failed to deliver in time for a family's vacation.

It seems that unintended consequences happen when the input into models is curated data, and the output is a black box. Regulating that is nearly impossible other than legal liability.

Explained decision

An explained decision is a fact-based statement followed by a conclusion. In modern computer lingo, it is called "a cognitive process of choices among alternatives." Explained decisions in Artificial Intelligence describe the data that was relied on and the programmed logic that most likely led to a given conclusion among choices. The computer itself can write decisions to explain logic- and data choices. That does not replace the human touch at all. In Artificial Intelligence explanations, secrecy is sometimes preferable to limit legal challenges. Attorneys may view explanations as self-indictments.

Some requirements apply to all cases, and especially to those involving autonomous systems.

- Applicable ethics principles have been identified, such as justice, truth, promise, right.
- A given dilemma has to be articulated, such as bias or unequal treatment among people.
- Available alternatives, beneficiaries, and victims.
- A decision comes with documentation and an explained rationale, including underlying assumptions.

Within the self-regulating FINRA community, explained decisions are a "right" for parties in arbitrated disputes. That Right is not automatic, but parties can jointly ask for it and pay for it with a small fee.

It can also happen that automated decisions are not explainable. Assume a process that starts with a vast database, runs on an amazingly fast computer, executes a self-learning (deep) algorithm, and then spits out a solution in the form of a black box. Black boxes, unlike in aviation, are systems with inputs and outputs that are not visible to the observer. The object for such an explained decision would be to state a possible cause-effect relationship, for which correlations are not suitable. While the explanation problem may remain unsolved for a while, the only moral behavior is publicly admitting temporary ignorance. In popular literature, this phenomenon is called "artificial ignorance," It can create trust more than making up a story can. An explained decision also needs to be grounded in ethical objectives. There are three approaches to start such a process for predictions, recommendation systems, and classifications.

In bisecting the word "prediction," consider "pre" as in before, and "diction" as in talking. Predictions are forecasts and, by definition, informed guesses. Some are better than others, and none are accurate all the time. Economists have a hard time predicting a single gross domestic product within 3%; newspapers often predict election outcomes as wishful thinking trumps statistics. Forecasts work well where the underlying patterns repeat themselves.

Forecasting is standard in sports betting, security pricing, health projection, and elections forecasting. Many forecasts are based on statistics and do not qualify as artificial intelligence. Some predictions depend on the mistaken assumptions in which a correlation becomes evidence for causation. It is not! Artificial Intelligence forecasting comes in three technologies: neural networks modeled after the human brain, machine learning (ML), supervised or unsupervised, and natural language processing (NLP) applied to written words. Many consumers would be awestruck by the amount of data that goes into a prediction and the speed at which predictions are made, such as in weather forecasting. Conventional predictions lack imagination and creativity and tend to fall outside of Artificial Intelligence.

Recommendation machines are ubiquitous. For example, customers who bought item X also bought a related item, Y. We, the supplier, therefore recommend that you go out and purchase those articles. The illogic is not the similarity but the biased conclusion. Both X and Y are humans, and both replace shoes and soap. Making such recommendations is neither unethical nor is it illegal, and it may be a customer convenience. As Big Data vendors use scaling, they create the problem of empty data cells and wrong data labels. The ethical issue is when wrong targets emerge from questionable data, sloppy labeling, and negligent management who do not test recommendations under stressful conditions before deploying them.

Classifications, or pattern recognition, in Artificial Intelligence also need to explain themselves when the answers are wrong, particularly to what degree they are wrong and how often they err. The underlying technologies are pattern recognition in combination with vision sensing. Well-known applications are facial recognition, raising serious ethical concerns. Autonomous vehicles continually classify many objects and make critical decisions based on what they "see." Less controversial are decisions like identifying plants, animals, photographs, and medical images, for example.

Control

The fundamental question to ask is this: Given all the capabilities of Artificial Intelligence that we humans now have and expect to have soon, ask not what *can* we do with this technology, but ask what *should* we do with it? It is mainly within our power to assure beneficial outcomes. Doing nothing or banning the entire technology is not an option. For one thing, the genie is out of the bottle by now. To even begin answering control questions, one needs to consider appropriate measurements for assessing risk. Once that is done, concentrate on finding a balance between benefit and harm. The pleasure/pain ratio is a measurement concept for happiness in the philosophy of hedonism.

The subject of control has a history, and like ethics itself, it dates back to the Greeks. Ktesibios (250 BC) made a water clock, a self-controlling machine, made especially useful by being "programable" with dials to tell time. It also functioned as an alarm clock. In our time, Norbert Wiener (1884-1964) wrote about control theory and embraced biological and mechanical principles made clear in a famous book on Cybernetics. Cybernetics refers to the communication and control of automatic machines and living things as well. Control Systems is a field of study of devices operating under their self-control, similar in principle to Ktesibios' alarm clock. Extending this concept to Artificial Intelligence means that algorithms are controlled without humans, with only a red panic button to stop a process. To achieve control over Artificial Intelligence, the idea of accountability has to take hold. So far, it is missing in action.

Being accountable is synonymous with being responsible. When the outcome is good, it means human happiness, fun, and money. If the effect is terrible, it means liability cost if caught. The mechanics of a control process may mimic seamen and airline pilots' practice. "I hear you; I understand you, and here is what I understood." Analyst/manager should practice dual project control and certify that a project supports the mission/vision statement, which is the ethical standard, by executing well. That is *to walk the talk*. If that sounds bureaucratic and expensive, it is. The alternatives are worse.

A diminished quality of human life would be a technology gone wrong. It could happen in the absence of ethical standards. Any application that limits human choices and increases dependencies on models can quickly turn people into lazy automatons who are forever dependent on this technology and its operators.

The rate of technological change affecting human customs and culture may also cause class conflict between an early adopter and late adopter, between the rich and relatively poor, and between full-time and underemployed workers. Alvin Toffler foresaw some of that that in his 1970 book *Future Shock.*

If Artificial Intelligence provides the public with what it wants and thereby be deemed moral, then is what the public wants itself ethical? There is no correct answer to this question, and besides, who is to judge? Humans can be aggressive by nature, and that pattern can be learned by machines now. Without human control, those machines can then run themselves.

Error prevention

All algorithms, robots, and models are subject to error. Errors themselves can be erroneous in the form of false positives or false negatives. A dramatic example is a story from 1983 when Stanislav Petrov, then a Lt. Col. in the then Soviet Union Army, detected incoming U.S. missiles on his radar and, in disbelief, hesitated to sound the alarm as required. He was a human being at the controls of a flawed control system that could have triggered another world war. He had the benefit of private education, not a Soviet military one. The potential consequences were hardly trivial. Above all, never hand over control to the machine alone!

Artificial Intelligence-based models that manage themselves and continually learn, adjust, and improve can manage error prevention and control. In the limit, could that process lead to a singularity? Probably not because technology lacks self-awareness and creative imagination. At the moment, Artificial Intelligence can create "art" like that of a Picasso, but it cannot create a Picasso equivalent.

Corporate culture is another challenging dimension affecting ethical outcomes. Some organizations like Berkshire Hathaway have it, while others, like Wells Fargo, used to have it. Culture is self-reliance, honesty, trust, and safety. Losing money due to competition or technology is not criminal and may be overcome with creativity and innovation. But losing a corporate reputation is quite often the end of the corporation. The risk of losing trust by dicey Artificial Intelligence technology is a near certainty in leading to a corporate demise. The responsibility for culture rests with a board of directors and the boards' communication of mission, vision, and values.

Data Monopolies

Corporate data monopoly is a potential threat to consumers, and it exists today in the form of Google, Amazon, Facebook, Apple. Are these monopolies legal or illegal, ethical, or unethical? It depends!

For an entity to qualify as a monopoly, it must have exclusive control of a product or service characterized by its ability to set prices, be a single seller, and put up a barrier to competitors' entry. If those conditions also harm consumers and economic success was obtained by unlawful methods, like blowing up competitors' oil wells, then it is illegal. The local electric company is a legal monopoly and most likely is regulated.

On the other hand, Apple, Amazon, and Walmart are close to monopolies as measured by market share and control. Being successful is not enough to make them illegal or unethical.

Biometrics

Any recognition- technology that defines human body attributes, human psychological descriptions, or trackable behavioral patterns of people- qualifies as biometric. That includes old-fashioned fingerprints, facial recognition, voice identifications methods, iris- or retina recognition, a persons' gate of walking, and even keyboarding patterns when writing. All of these recognition technologies are subject to natural errors. Most of the time, a combination of those attributes serves identifications purposes. Used in combination for increased security, if one feature is unreliable, the combination becomes unreliable. In the literature, this is called "soft biometrics." A suitable synonym for soft biometrics is "junk science."

Take *Clearview A.I.*, a U.S. company that matches facial images to names, via a database of three billion pictures obtained from the Internet without anybody knowing it. Clearview then sells surveillance tools to both police departments and private concerns. From there, these data could travel into the data-ether to be combined with more data and produce even more dodgy results. Clearview is not the only nontransparent vendor in the world. Companies like that do not grow organically due to natural demand for this information; they succeed because of government funding and general insecurity in industry and society. Financial incentives often outclass ethics. However, contingent liability regulation may put a temporary restraint on the more abusive practices.

CHAPTER 6
ETHICS SELF-REGULATION IN PRACTICE

Technology self-regulation does not just address one company or several of them; it does not even address any industry in particular, and indeed not merely one sector of an economy. It addresses the entire technology of Artificial Intelligence as seen today and tomorrow, affecting all humanity on this planet.

.Regulating industrial life is a serious matter of our time. Individuals do self-control based on beliefs and culture. Companies commit to values enumerated in their public pronouncements, industries like chemicals, forest products, and nuclear power have moral principles and standards designed for their members, often only in the form of guidelines. Take the Responsible Care Program, for instance. It was initiated in Canada in 1985 and defined voluntary safety-, health, and environmental standards for the chemical industry. More than 100 of the world's largest chemical companies endorsed those standards. Their combined capacity covered 90% of the industry. However, a small group of those member companies did not comply and got caught in very public controversies, thereby creating mistrust for the entire industry and the Responsible Care Program. An ethical collapse of only a few players in this technology could sink all of us.

Without an actual enforcement mechanism, voluntary alignment to moral standards, the technology of Artificial Intelligence will most likely experience a similar fate. Attempting to self-regulate an evolving technology, rather than only an industry, is a relatively new concept. Under self-regulation, practitioners would theoretically commit to abiding by a private/public code designed to prevent terrible outcomes. Private/public suggest that industry and government are not in competition when it comes to ethics.

On the contrary, the relationship between technology and the central government is more like a continuum. Here, private self-regulation is field-testing the rules, and the government writes them, and the rest of us may flourish.

Self-regulation has many benefits, one of which is responding to problems in time, e.g., what should we do where facial recognition technology gets it all wrong? How flexible are the practitioners of this technology to respond to any problem, and how sensitive? Many aspects of Artificial Intelligence are experimental, and pass muster as a good thing. The Center for Disease Control (CDC) requires extensive proof before certifying a medication for public consumption. In Artificial Intelligence, we do not have that requirement for efficacy. Proof of concept should become a moral standard, and it should be available.

The corresponding negative of self-regulation is the public perception that self-regulation is flawed. The worst of history will repeat itself with shady characters at the control button. However, that need not be the case when the regulated and regulators are on the same page, and the regulation process is democratic. The vision is for ethics improvement now, with ethics perfection a distant goal.

Wanted: A technological morality standard for Artificial Intelligence

Easy, a casual observer might say "State values most of us already have, write rules, come up with quantitative measures, and enforce". One can program most of that into algorithms, and voila, ethics is automatic. But money and power are at stake, and management can get emotional.

An Artificial Intelligence moral code should exist before self-regulating it becomes possible. The best time to develop such code is from public failures. That may look a bit counter-intuitive, but fear propels action. In 2013 an IBM algorithm, run on its over-promoted Watson supercomputer, made unsafe recommendations for cancer treatments, causing a pause in treatments. Amazon dropped its recruitment machine-learned models because all they did was repeat well-established biases in hiring, primarily men. Apple tried and failed to replace a phone fingerprint identification scheme with a face-recognition version in which a mask easily fooled it. Failures are not per se bad; in fact, they can be instructive. But a public perception that this technology is morally a runaway makes this moment precisely the time to institute an antidote. Such an antidote is a code of self-regulation naturally leading to fairly legislated rules.

A normative framework for this technology more or less exists. Most people agree that privacy, human health, safe transportation, and nearly full employment are essential goals. The habit of saying, "this is the way we do it around here," is passee by now. Instead, a re-think/re-engineering approach is the expected norm. In a free market, private and public parochial institutions will naturally fall by the wayside. That is a good thing and perhaps a contributing factor for Artificial Intelligence advancing so fast. But a technology-aided concentration without a moral code could reintroduce unhealthy economic conditions.

Wanted: New institutions to guide Artificial Intelligence ethics

Only a few institutions could come close to regulating Artificial Intelligence ethics in the western world today. Many institutions display a regulatory interest, but few have the regulatory authority or are willing to invest. There are; however, new self-regulatory mechanisms bubbling up.

AAAI, founded in 1979, is the Association for the Advancement of Artificial Intelligence. It is an industry trade membership organization that promotes understanding of the technology, encourages research, and provides guidance and educational resources. Recent conference papers suggest that regulating ethics is too early and culturally nearly impossible on a global scale.

ITU is the International Telecommunications Union, founded in 1865. It traditionally regulates radio frequencies worldwide. It also has a non-regulatory interest to influence Artificial Intelligence with an *AI For Good* program. Theoretically, it could help formulate ethics standards. Being part of the United Nations System, it is likely to be a case of too many cooks in the kitchen, 193 nation-cooks to be exact.

ACM is the Association of Computing Machinery, founded in 1947; it is a collective membership voice that embraces, provides, inspires computing without regulating anything. However, it is a reputable source for research on the "how-to" regulate ethics question.

IEEE is the Institute for Electrical and Electronics Engineers. Founded in 1963, it is, as the words imply, a professional membership organization. It aims to create benefits, improves trust, is pro-growth, and seeks to serve humans. Artificial Intelligence is within its purview.

ISO is the International Organization for Standards, created in 1947. Its work applies more to goods and services than to technologies. ISO could be an influential mover and shaker in the quest for ethical standards in technologies. ISO is a role model for self-regulation and standards development. There is a business folk- wisdom that says, "the people who get you in trouble are not the same people who can get you out of trouble." In a contrarian line of reasoning, the people who succeed in writing standards for physical products could also be the same who can write standards for ethics in brand new technologies.

OpenAI is a San Francisco-based research and development company governed by the not-for-profit OpenAI LP. The organization dedicates itself to Artificial General Intelligence (AGI), emphasizing autonomous systems outperforming humans and promotes long-term safety and public benefit. Noteworthy in this context is that it does not have to sell anything and is free to promote the public good. OpenAI could be a valuable participant for self-imposed ethical standards, but not necessarily enforcing them through self-regulation. The organization was founded and funded by Elon Musk and others in 2015.

These institutions share the ability to contribute to self-regulated ethical standards, which neither can do alone. The option of laissez-faire capitalism and leaving standards open to interpretation is dangerous. The likelihood of the government coming to the rescue before something damaging happening is unrealistic. Self-interest is neither illegal nor is it immoral. The Scottish philosopher Adam Smith defined capitalism in his 1776 published thesis called The Wealth of Nations. He stated that the sum of everybody's self-interest creates a social good in the form of an "invisible hand." The "invisible hand" is the social good resulting from self-interested parties. For example, consumers can enjoy fresh raspberries for breakfast in the winter because another person makes a living growing them in the winter. Others pick them in return for wages, and somebody with an airplane will fly those raspberries to market for a reasonable and customary fee. What would be objectionable is price-fixing enabled Artificial Intelligence.

Arguments against self-regulation exist, and some are reasonable. Once self-regulators are in charge, they could become monopolistic authoritarians themselves, a bit like the old Dutch Guilds used to be.

Where we are now

One of the current positives is that 96 nations in the world are democracies. Change and adjustments are possible as countries have the built-in capacity to adjust. The current negative is that 95 other nations are autocratically governed. Democratic governments can address a moral vacuum by reflecting, debating, voting, regulating, and adapting. Technological self-regulation has a fair chance of taking hold in democratic societies. Autocratic ones, on the other hand, live in fear of their population. While investing heavily and using the tools of this technology, their purposes can be a lot more sinister.

There is no single mechanism to address many of the risks associated with this technology because the need for risk assessment did not arise until the potential threats became apparent. To start proposing a normative moral standard, one must lean on historical references of impeccable authority, if for no other reason than to preempt the camp of nay-sayers a chance to say nay. One such document is The Declaration of Human Rights, adopted in 1948 by the United Nations General Assembly in Paris. It has 30 articles, and here are just a few of them to guide a moral framework for Artificial Intelligence. In abbreviated form and listed by Article number are nine of those articles tweaked to the technology of Artificial Intelligence:

Article 1: All humans are free and equal in the eyes of the law.
The technology must not constrain peoples' freedom.

Article 3: Right to liberty, freedom, security.
The technology must not compromise security, freedom.

Article 6: Recognition as a person.
The technology cannot remake humans into automatons.

Article 9: Arbitrary arrests.
Facial recognition technology still gets it wrong and does harm.

Article 12: Right to privacy.
The technology can help to be forgotten and remembered; it supports and hinders.

Article 16: Protection of family by State.
States can become arbiters of morality.

Article 19: Right to have opinions.
It does not mean shouting "fire" in a theatre.

Article 23: Right to work.
Must be adjusted for robotics, universal income.

Article 26: Right to education.
Girl child is equal to boy child.

Another moral role model for Artificial Intelligence in the United Nations Charter. The UN is a forum for every nation on the planet to have a seat and be heard, an outlet to blow off steam that can lead to settlements. Self-regulation can work similarly on a nano level. The idea is to blow off steam and settle on something that works. A statute depicting swords turning into plowshares is in the UN garden at its New York headquarters. "We The People" must have a voice in how the technology of Artificial Intelligence is allowed to affect our lives.

A Moral Code for the Free World

Traditionally when a significant social problem arises, the reaction is to change the law, as was US Social Security in 1935. The case considered in these pages is in anticipation of significant upheaval.

The question is, where to start? We have the historical precedent of the Dartmouth conference mentioned earlier. A similar initiative may be a way to get started. But in this field valid reasons for wanting to sit at the table? Good candidates are trade associations like AAAI, ACM, IEEE, ISO, having undertaken studies and being interested in Artificial Intelligence. Also, FINRA matters based on quasi self-regulatory experience and in rule writing and representing the mission of fraud prevention. ISO is also self-regulatory and has experience in standards development.

Companies with Artificial Intelligence software platforms from which their clients develop their applications without having to start anew. The obvious suspects are Apple, Amazon, Alphabet, and OpenAI. Additional entities may come from industrial sectors like pharmaceuticals and companies that create automated processes.

Given the historical precedent, academic institutions like the Massachusetts Institute of Technology, the University of Southern California, and Dartmouth College are appropriate. A mix with smaller educational institutions is appropriate since talent is more dispersed now than it used to be.

A neutral foundation may help balance the design of ethics standards for technologies in Artificial Intelligence. In the 1956 Dartmouth conference case, the Rockefeller Foundation was the sponsor for the 10-day summer event.

Not even ethicists are immune to conflict of interest. There is no better proof than a case of an ethics transgression committed in the name of ethics. A US accounting firm ranked #2 among its peers of 50 firms worldwide is a case in point. It publishes a report "Thriving in the era of pervasive AI" for three years in a row. The story is an annual survey addressing risk, governance, and ethics. The version from July 14th, 2020, cites the good ethics news of a major German industrial firm for training 20,000 software engineers and executives between now and 2025 to use Artificial Intelligence with a curriculum that includes its code of ethics. Now hear this! In 2019, said firm paid a $100 million penalty for pollution cheating software it sold mostly to automobile firms. Its website touted the use of Artificial Intelligence to fight pollution, its own history notwithstanding. Coming fully around the ethics circle, said private giant accounting firm is the auditor. In simple terms, the foxes are in charge of the chicken coups feigning to serve the common good with their home-certified Artificial Intelligence standards.

Flowery language and foggy definitions give the appearance of advanced ethics but are insufficient. An example of a code makes the following abbreviated five points. Parentheses are author's, as are italics.

1. The code of ethics *should* reflect an *invented for life ethos* with a *quest* for innovation and social responsibility. (the term *ethos* means a culture of aspiring to something)

2. Automated decisions *should* have a human arbiter (*"must"* would be a more emphatic statement, but who is that social arbiter person? Does that person have the power to say "no"?)

3. Safe, robust, and explainable decisions

4. Trust

5. Meet *legal* requirements (as if that were an option)

One must expect that developing a moral code for Artificial Intelligence technologies will entail long debates before something concrete is on paper. Let that debate start with the concept of self-regulation by two organizations, one for most of us and the other for the rest of us.

Organization #1 Self-regulating ethics standards (NGO)

The ethics under scrutiny pertain to technology and not to a set of companies or an industrial sector or political concentrations. Hypothetically, ethical standards applicable for that technology fall into two parts, those who favor ethics standards and those who do not. All those in favor will organize to create- and observe those standards. All those opposed will have a chance to explain their opposition publicly to an advocate of good ethics.

The current state of business ethics art is this:

1. We know from history how to define ethical conduct; by humans, government, and corporations. Agreeing on standards, while not easy, should therefore be possible.

2. The technologies of Artificial Intelligence are evolving, and evolution has no final destinations as far as anybody knows. But in the immediate term, ethics standards have to be responsive to society's current needs.

3. Democracies have the built-in feature for compromise and adjustments. Central planning is the opposite and not an option.

4. Society expects that this new technology may simultaneously do significant harm and be helpful to humans.

5. In contrast to past industrial movements, this one is coming faster

than prior ones.

6. We can learn a great deal from existing self-regulatory institutions and adopt their best practices.

We can learn from patently unethical corporations. Preferably court-certified, to understand what to avoid and incorporate that knowledge into standards.

Both approaches, promoting technological benefit and avoiding technical harm, define better ethics, the good and the bad, the Yin and Yang dualism. A dual metaphor relates to the safety of bank vaults. Both the robbers' skills and the bank's skills to protect clients define the standard for safety.

A mechanism for generally acceptable standards requires the formation of two non-governmental organizations. One convincing corporations to flourish on ethics and trust, and the other compelling corporations to recognize the hopelessness of violating trust.

- The first organization is a self-regulatory membership not-for-profit entity focused on best ethics practices and a commitment to legal compliance by its members. It also fosters creating standards and methods for members with ISO as role models.

- The second organization opposes technology abuse, a first responder of intentional or accidental bad outcomes. Also, its public service is in issue identification and awareness, litigation support, mediation, ombudsman services, including name and shame as the last resort. It can also be a service for regulators and law enforcement. It intends to be an agent of change and not an agent in policing ethics.

Two non-governmental organizations have different objectives, and they are independent of each other. The reason for the two organizations is this: It would be a conflict of interest for one entity to serve those purposes under the same management. Standards and value definitions, one hopes, will emerge over time. The spirit of moving forward is not top-down legislation of ethics standards from a fatherly all-knowing central authority, but bottom-up insights derived from working experiences in the fields.

	NGO 1 For Standards	NGO 2 Ethics Ombudsman
Objective	Guide good AI outcomes for members and society. Create trust and, thereby, value for members. Develop- and adopt ethics standards.	Minimize negative AI outcome Ethics AI watchdog Private/public alternative ethics dispute resolution
Organized as	Non-government organization (NGO) not for profit corporation International reach Centrally owned	A non-governmental organization (NGO} Not for profit\ corporation International reach Regionally owned
Funding Mechanism	membership fees initial foundation grants research, publications, education No obligation to sell anything.	Foundation grants State- and Federal government research Alternative dispute resolution No obligation to sell anything.
Market	All scientific and commercial sectors companies deploying AI technologies Academic institutions	All scientific and commercial legal entities
Governance	Corporate Board with a term limit Board represented by members and funders.	Citizen Board with term limits A board representing law, academic, citizen
Accountable to	Membership Society	Society Law
Relations to Government	Supports/influences legislation Suggests rules and standards	Whistleblowing Supports enforcement
Dispute Resolution	Private, internal, non-judicial mediation Persuasion	Persuasion Voluntary third - party arbitration/mediation Name and shame
Products-Services	Ethics compliance certification Ethics standards development Publications, case studies, research reports Private/public meetings Assist members with compliance.	Brings dodgy AI ethics to public attention. Mediates solutions for better AI ethics. Public position papers Conferences Case studies and research

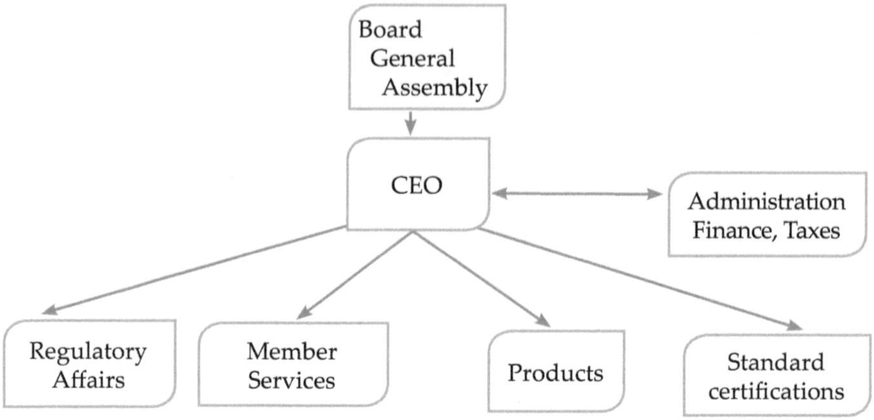

Figure 6.1: *NGO 1 For Standards*

Board

At organizing time zero, the original members, like the 1956 Dartmouth group, will have a plan, a few supporting member corporations, and initial funding in place. In addition, the group will have a certificate of incorporation in a US State, a small checking account, and most importantly, verbal encouragement from a wide range of industry sources. At a minimum, the Boards' composition reflects foundation supporters, academics, industries. Board member terms should be relatively short, with a one-term potential renewal subject to a staggered election. Board members are to receive customary and reasonable compensation in expectation for their service. This venture is not a charitable volunteer effort.

Chief Operating officer

This person is the persona of the mission. They must have an innate ability to sell abstract concepts. When visiting the Hill in Washington DC, such a person should have a > 50% chance of running into at least one former colleague. The immediate goal is to reach a critical mass in membership and maximize ethical standards' development and adoption.

Administration

The first administrative task is finance, accounting for membership fees and expenses, financial planning, budgets, and grant-writing. True independence comes when membership income pays all bills, and grants are not needed.

Membership services

Any activities that support members in the adoption of ethical standards belong in this category. At a minimum, these include legal measures to adopt- and publish and then help the membership comply. A small standard for a niche technology should be easier to achieve than finding the equivalent to an ISO standard. Showing small successes early gets the show on the road. A byproduct of crafting ethics standards are likely to be case studies and databases for publications and training. For example, cases that simultaneously comply with contradictory legislation of the European GDPR rules and the State of California rules.

Ethics standards: research & development

For all practical purposes, no ethical standards exist to govern the technologies of Artificial Intelligence in particular. Those standards have to be developed collaboratively from some of the principles introduced in these pages. This NGO-1 organization is the prime mover. The process should include representation from technology innovators and technology clients plus ordinary citizens with no emotional attachments to the subject in question. Let us not repeat a world in which only medical doctors rule on health, only lawyers rule on governance, and only movie critics tell everybody what the next show you must see is. Recommendations for standards are then field-tested and adjusted for a legal review, a vote, temporary adoption, documentation, and rule writing. The process from innovation to ethical standards is a very long one. It has to be a long one for citizens to stay safe.

To put the preceding paragraph into context, consider the following application: An autoregressive language model called GPT-3 uses deep-learning to produce text. Should there be an ethical rule in the publishing industry to identify any GPT-3 generated text?

Public and regulatory affairs

This office maintains liaison with Federal and State ethics initiatives and informs members of new developments and requirements. It communicates legislative changes to its members via newsletters or webinars. Conversely, this office also tells State and Federal ethics legislative offices of industry concerns through a properly open channel, rather than the customary well-funded lobbying through third parties. This office's mission puts industry and government into a cooperative framework, rather than in an adversarial one, as was the case in the past. Both parties gain.

Organization #2 The Ethics Ombudsman (NGO)

Making the reasonable assumption that misconduct with Artificial Intelligence tools can happen in the marketplace, this organization aims to address the negative side of the ethics coin.

Associations that advocate for causes are many. The Children's Defense Fund, The National Alliance for Mental Illness, are examples. So is The Alliance for Justice, an association of 120 associations that coordinate efforts on common issues. Usually, a new association gets off the ground when a leading group of persons takes the initiative, as was the case with the American Enterprise Institute, a policy think-tank founded in 1938 by a businessman named Louis Brown. Similarly, it was also the case for the Aspen Institute, founded in 1949 by Walter Päpke with a mission for arts and culture. Some funding came from foundations like the Carnegie-, Rockefeller-, and now Gates foundations. Another case is that of the American Enterprise Institute, funded by corporations and by individuals. Closer to home is the Association for Artificial Intelligence (AAAI). A far-sighted group of people created it with a significant endowment in the 1990s to do its work. The AAAI has an extensive code of ethics which, on the surface, pushes all the right buttons but fails as an enforcement mechanism. Unlike ISO quality standards that convey commercial value, AAAI ethics provisions suggest voluntary compliance without having teeth in the marketplace.

To serve diverse communities, the US Federal government maintains regional offices. A similar local organization is appropriate to help various commercial regions advocate for settlement on this technology's ethical standards. Ethical tolerances likely vary by region, and dispute settlements coming from one location, like Washington DC, appear too authoritarian to be readily accepted. Consider California, replicate that experience over the remaining six regions, and start a sister organization for the EU. One of the UK and Commonwealth nations to establish the first office.

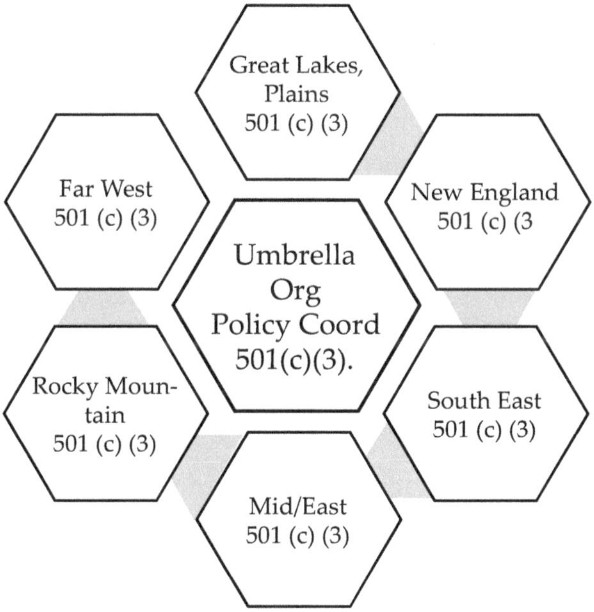

Figure 6.2: *Regional Artificial Intelligence Ombudsman Ethics Organization*

The group of six will oppose unethical practices in Artificial Intelligence- associated technologies. Committed individuals regionally own the six groups, central managed, and with voluntary associations to similar international entities. Neither of NGO1 nor NGO2 shares any connection. They are legally separate and distinct from each other. There are multiple reasons for proposing a regional organization with regional citizen ownership. One is to have local parties address local ethics, and the other is to have local inputs to local ethics concerns. A centralized approach to business ethics risks failure for no other reason than central planning has natural limits. For example, the phrase *I am from the government, and I am here to help* captures the sentiment. Six regional Artificial Intelligence ombudsman organizations share policy, vision, objectives, and collaboration. A Better Ethics Business Bureau, fine-tuned for Artificial Intelligence ethics, is the reference here.

1. The New England region to be composed of Connecticut, Maine, Massachusetts, New Hampshire, Rhode Island, and Vermont.

2. The Mideast region includes Delaware, the District of Columbia, Maryland, New Jersey, New York, and Pennsylvania.

3. The Great Lakes region comprises Illinois, Indiana, Michigan, Ohio, and Wisconsin.

4. Plains region is composed of Iowa, Kansas, Minnesota, Missouri, Nebraska, North Dakota, and South Dakota,

5. The Southeast region includes Alabama, Arkansas, Florida, Georgia, Kentucky, Louisiana, Mississippi, North Carolina, South Carolina, Tennessee, Virginia, and West Virginia.

6. The Southwest region to be composed of Arizona, New Mexico, Oklahoma, and Texas.

7. The Rocky Mountain region includes Colorado, Idaho, Montana, Utah, and Wyoming.

8. The Far West region to be composed of California, Hawaii, Alaska, Nevada, Oregon, and Washington. In summary form, the following picture emerges:

Alternative conflict resolution

The Umbrella organization will have to provide each office with training so that on the first day, staff will have a lot more work to do than show up. For example, The Great Lakes/Plains office will face somewhat different issues than the Southeast office. For one thing, The Great Lakes office will have to understand BIPA, a State of Illinois law called the Biometric Information Privacy Act. Biometrics capture human behavioral characteristics for identification. Included are not only routine fingerprints but also facial images and cadence, as well as voice identification. BIPA grants the right to private action, which is the right for individuals to sue in a court of law. That fact alone is a corporate attention-getter and has stopped ill-conceived technology investments in Illinois from moving forward.

An example would be an individual described as having a confident baritone voice, together with high cheekbones and a slight limp, all of which match a suspect. Distinguishing an evil eye- from a benevolent one could be next. That is a dangerous prospect for society, and it falls under the rubric of bad science.

Each regional office is likely to share facts surrounding what triggered an ethics investigation. Local offices may share their respective databases. In combination, a nationwide and comprehensive database of Artificial Intelligence ethics cases evolves into being a handy research tool. Humans are inclined to build new social structures on top of existing ones. Our new ethics advocates could lean on Better Business Bureau- and Medicines Sans Frontier's frameworks to model their operations. Accountability will start early with the sharing of reliable cases with the public and with governments. For instance, how many ethics cases are on the docket, their nature and magnitude, meetings held, the number- and nature of conflicts settled or addressed.

CHAPTER 7
RE-ENGINEERING OUR COMMON FUTURE

Self-Regulating Artificial Intelligence ethics has to start from somewhere; the idea needs a spark to get going. That spark, the grand vision perhaps, has to come from a community of visionaries who see both problems and opportunities at the same time. In the short term, the need is to avert inequities resulting from the absence of standards. In the long term, the loss of human control over the technology is the issue.

In the absence of standards, nearly everything is permitted!

The condition of no standards is to be avoided!

Time is of the essence!

Society is well-conditioned to understand that actions have consequence, and all of that can lead to the imposition of rewards and punishment. But, so do incentives when engineered into commerce. Then the imposition of punishment is minimal. The odds of commercial successes resulting from compliance to standards must be large. Conversely, the odds of commercial failure resulting from non-compliance must be overwhelming. The puzzle to solve is this: Begin to define technology standards that promote stability and trust in commerce. Next, work on incentives for voluntary compliance to standards, and then keep going.

Traditionally, legislated regulation is a response to a publicly perceived need. For example, something goes wrong in a given technology, and a wide swath of the population is outraged and expresses their anger via social media and demonstrations for the evening news. Elected- and unelected politicians see an opportunity and jump on the bandwagon and start drafting rules and hold hearings, and more. That lengthy process is then followed by correcting the original misalignments accompanied by an allocation of spoils among the movers and shakers in the form of money and jobs. That is the accepted price of democracy and in itself not all bad. All the while the technologies are roaring onward with innovations. The process from initiating legislative changes to its eventual passing and being enforced, is simply too long in the case of Artificial Intelligence. Too many things can go awry in that time interval.

Self-regulation is the only feasible alternative to fill this current ethics vacuum. Self- regulation is also a leading contributor for earlier- and better legislation. There are two precedents, namely OSHA and Climate Change.

How OSHAs began from private initiatives

A response to a profound industrial need is found in the narrative leading up to the formation of the Occupational, Safety, and Health Administration (OSHA). The Industrial Revolution of the late 19th Century lured many rural citizens into poor working conditions in cities. A very similar phenomenon occurred in the 20th Century in Communist China. The 19th Century US version was accompanied by a high accident rate. Industrial dumping of waste materials contributed to poor health of workers. On one hand, the Industrial Revolution was beneficial for workers in terms of wages, and to consumers for useful new products at reasonable prices. Similarly, Artificial Intelligence provides many new conveniences and assists workers on their job. In comparison, the technology of Artificial Intelligence is now at a stage similar to where workers were around 1880, in that there are threats on the horizon, albeit rather different. OSHA's history in review looks like this:

> 1877 Massachusetts passes the first safety law for workers, it pertained to ventilation in factories. It was a response to very observable health issues.
>
> 1913 US President Taft signs the paperwork to create the US Department of Labor. A case of politics catching up with society.
>
> In 1945 WWII ends, and production returns to meet civilian needs, factory worker conditions were poor at the time, work-related accidents increased dramatically, and the chemical- and steel sectors of the economy polluted the ground and the air.
>
> 1970 US President Nixon signs the OSHA Act, which is dedicated to worker safety standards. The estimated industrial accident rate at the time stood at 14,000 workers killed out of 130 million employed. The mining, transportation and chemical sectors

accounted for many of those fatalities.

It took almost 100 years for legislation to respond to bad working conditions. How long will it take for legislation to respond to unacceptable outcomes in the technology of Artificial Intelligence? In bringing about a change, a lot of private events in-between contributed to the build-up of the momentum. For example, inspections of factories in Massachusetts 1877, machine guard railings 1977, a West Virginia coal mine accident in 1907 had 362 fatalities, several States issued rules containing many loopholes. The Russell Sage Foundation, a private non-profit social science research organization, issued a paper known as the Pittsburgh Survey, describing working conditions in Allegheny County coal mines at the time. In a somewhat related development, the concept of workers compensation was already operational in Germany under Otto von Bismarck since 1884. Workers compensation became law in Wisconsin in 1921. Progress was slow in cases of human disfiguration from phosphorus in the chemical industry, from lung cancer caused by working in coal mines, and from lead pollution in steel smelters. The law changed not entirely because of public outrage, not because of opposition from industry worried with cost, but mostly from a coincidental political alignment between the Democrat and Republican parties in a US election year. According to George Guenther, OSHA's director at the time, labor union supported the issue to compensate for their decline in membership, Democrats supported it as a matter of a pro-labor tradition , and Republicans did not oppose it because it was a presidential election year and bipartisanship was good public relations.

The lesson learned is this: with Artificial Intelligence we do not have the leisure of so many years to come up with ethics standards. Waiting for bad things to happen before addressing the problem is dangerous. Relying on a solely political solution to come to the rescue, carries unfavorable odds, a conventional legislative reform process is too time consuming and subject to compromise. Compromising on ethics can lead to anything. This new technology needs new institutions to deal with standards and ethics, self-regulation may be the best available alternative start.

How climate change began from public initiatives

Ethics issues arise from climate change, which grossly simplified, appears now as a matter of carbon-dioxide in the air causing our planet to warm, with fractions of a degrees having mostly adverse consequences. Poor people living in low elevation areas may suffer first and more than others.

There are of course differences between Artificial Intelligence and climate change. Climate Change's crowning regulatory achievement was the United Nations' sponsored Kyoto Protocol of 1992. That agreements' objective is to reduce the carbon dioxide emission rate for 191 nations that signed up. The outcome so far is that some nations succeeded, some tried and failed, others cheated. The USA never committed much to begin with, and in fact withdrew in altogether in 2001. China is exempt from the agreement because it is a "developing nation" and ditto for India. China, India, and the USA comprise 38 percent of the world's 7.8 billion human souls. In the meantime, Global CO2 emissions have now reached 400 ppm, the highest level in 800 years and the average world temperature is up 1 degree Celsius over pre-industrial times. Ironically, concurrent with attempts to regulate climate through governmental action and international agreements, the technology of electric cars, power generation without or less coal and oil, battery storage, are all signs that industry and technology are responding to the problem. Responding to the problem is not the same as solving the problem. Industry in this case is a private actor. The solution to the problem of climate change will take both public and private parties.

A casual observer will notice a few thinking opportunities on AI ethics:

- Efforts to deal with existential technology problems started with a few academics, that is private, and the technology's control is now moving towards the legislation realm, and that is public.

- Climate problems were first recognized in a major way by institutions like The United Nations. The issue now has broad street level private support.

- Both Climate Change and Artificial Intelligence ethics are hard to manage. In climate, we try to prevent bad things from happening, and in technology we promote good things to happen.

Given this somewhat hopeless assessment of our lot, it seems best then to accept our limitations in wanting to control everything, and instead adapt and make the best of that without giving up.

And now the future begins

We The People have a history of trying to regulate our world to the extent humanly possible. Our ability to handle is subject to mostly physical limits, and many others as well. Concerning Artificial Intelligence, we face a ubiquitous technology that requires a different approach than was the case for Spinning Jennies, steam engines, and electricity. For one thing, the subject matter is not a political movement, not about a sector of the economy, and not an industry or a group of commercial companies. It is a technology, and there is not a single entity from which we must wrestle control.

We The People manage this technology and control it for our benefits, otherwise it will control us. Left alone, whatever happens can become irreversible. Together, that is academics, industry and government plus private initiatives, can sort this out together for mutual benefit.

CHAPTER 8
MEASURING ETHICS

The nature of measurements

"If you cannot measure it, you cannot control it," is business folk wisdom sounding genuine and convincing. But when it comes to AI technology, are ethics measurable? Even if measurable, controllability adds another layer of unknowns. If we define the word "control" to include the influencing of outcomes, then the answer is affirmative. It may seem semantic nit-picking, but the word "control" also conjures up images of meeting goals at all costs. We wish to control Artificial Intelligence technologies to remain in many human hands and benefit many humans for this instant case. We want to avoid a situation where only a few actors govern certain technologies for the benefit of those few. That, it appears, is the direction the industry is now heading. To get this measurement problem right, it calls for new sets of metrics different from older conventions. For example, any new metrics regimen has to tackle the peculiarities of quantum computing, autonomous machines, supper-intelligence, robotics everywhere, 5G communications, virtual reality, Big Data, and more.

Adjudicating evolving technologies is especially hard because we need to know who benefits and who gets hurt to be ethically accountable. Industrial statesmanship requires trying in that direction. There are great incentives of not even asking the who-gets-hurt question, much less measure it. Looking back at the history of measurements for guidance is not sufficient for meaningful answers. This chapter aims to lay the groundwork for developing metrics that meet the current- and future needs.

The need for measuring ethics does come up in many academic Artificial Intelligence conferences. Here it becomes a challenge for which there is no solution. Then attendees go home only to return next year with more concerns. The reasons for postponements range from the world is too diverse for a unified approach, some methods were tried before and failed, or perhaps soon computer algorithms may be able to do ethics by themselves? It is undoubtedly true that algorithms can do much of that, but not all of it. That would violate the cardinal rule of having humans control the panic button at all times.

A fundamental definition of measurement describes the size, dimension, capacity, proportion, or judgment. This definition applies to length, weight, volume, time, mathematics formulae, physics, music, law, and endless endeavors. We live in a culture obsessed with seeking precision, and we use numbers to make it happen. Once we have it, we feel in control. If the numbers are what we expect, we feel good and reward ourselves for achieving those numbers. Such numbers can represent our cholesterol, a test score for a professional certificate, low calories from the last lunch, a high return on our investment, price-earnings ratio, the latest customer satisfaction survey results over the Internet, and more. Of these, length is the oldest measure, and it arose out of the need to survey land ownership as soon as property rights became law. One can argue that most measurements arise from a physical need to have them. For example, an inch is a thumb; a foot is self-explanatory; a yard is a human pace, and a mile is one thousand paces, or what the Romans called *milie passus*.

If a machine exhibits intelligent behavior indistinguishable from human behavior, most people will agree that we are dealing with artificial intelligence. Alan Turing established measurement for machine intelligence as early as 1950, and that concept remains valid. Roughly stated, if a human person can't tell whether a response to a question came from a fellow human or a machine, machine intelligence has been displayed. Whether that intelligence is good, bad, or indifferent remains unanswered. Finding ethical standards for machine intelligence comes up in connection with technologies like 5-G-communications, quantum computing, machines that learn, neural networks, to name a few. Emerging from the digital industrial revolution, revolution number 3, we rely on numbers to help with ethical conflicts. An example of that is the efficacy of a new medication. It is good if it is a cure; it is probably OK if the drug's efficacy is 95%. The term "efficacy" means formal and under ideal conditions, while "effectiveness" means under field conditions, which is usually a lower number. To further complicate the search for ethics metrics, consider Artificial Intelligence products or services that (a) affects women differently than men, that (b) accidentally or deliberately discriminate on the grounds of race or age, (c) social media that produces fake literature, (d) accounting methods that lend themselves to hide or distort conclusions, (d) governmental reporting from a political class, that manufactures certainty where none exists, (e) privacy issues applied to EU citizens that differ for US citizens with which international firms have to comply with, and (f) nepotism as it is practiced by autocrats worldwide? One can conclude from these facts that ethics in Artificial Intelligence is a largely unresolved issue needing immediate attention. A lingering ethics vacuum may lead to more abuse within a relatively short time. Humans will be the losers in the absence of standards. Yes, machines can learn a lot, do a lot, and help us improve life on earth. But machines can, so far at least, not understand anything, a fact one should take comfort in.

The measurability of AI-ethics

At this point, it is safe to say that the technology of Artificial Intelligence is ushering in a new industrial age and that society needs new metrics to manage it. Current behavioral standards in the industry do not address some of the unique problems that are emerging.

Now What? A laissez-faire attitude dependent on goodwill by industry is perilous. The existence of decency may be without question, but new temptations resulting from this technology are overwhelming. One has to assume that good people sometimes do not remain as good as they started. A benevolent technology dictator who understands everything coming to the rescue is not realistic. So, where are we now, and how do we proceed to meet new demands?

Table 8.1: *Ethical metrics*

Organization	Mission	Principle Ethic	Metrics
ISO	Quality standards for products and services	Safety, value, quality	A quality process implies a quality product., ergo, measure the process
Amnesty International	Prevent injustices	Human rights	Case law, name-shame, over time
Rotary International	Community Service	Self-reliance	Charitable deeds and funding Membership community
Carnegie Endowment for Peace	Cooperation for peace between nations	Create timely solutions for problems	Publications and conferences cases
American Red Cross	Protect life and health in war and peace	Non-discrimination for victims	50% of US blood supply, survival teaching, support for military veterans
Oxfam	Prevention of poverty and related injustices	Exercise the power of people	Candid stakeholder reporting for its operations

Industrial ethics issues can arise anywhere at any time, and how our predecessors handled their problems at their time may give us a clue how we can control our current affairs now. What are some common denominators from the past that can guide us now?

1. All of the above-listed institutions represent private initiatives in response to a then-current societal problem.

2. All cases embody limited self-governance. ISO and OSHA support regulations; Amnesty International supports the same human rights enshrined in the US Constitution and the United Nations Charter; the work of Rotary International benefits communities in ways local government cannot.

3. Oxfam works on reducing poverty and the abuses resulting from it. Apart from relief, its work also covers consciousness-raising for a complacent population.

4. None of these organizations oppose legislation. The American Red Cross, for example, has been a role model for responding to emergencies for 139 years now.

Reenforcing the self-regulation case made in Chapter 4.

1. Create NGOs (non-governmental organizations) to establish ethical standards its members voluntarily accept and practice, thereby creating value for themselves in the public's eyes. There's no lack of candidates who want to lead the pack in the hope of gaining market value, that is, trust, among their customers. The bad operators who do not play by any rules will face another NGO acting more like Oxfam. In combination, these two NGOs can react quickly to protect humans from technological abuse.

2. Let new standards in AI ethics rapidly evolve from industry cases, rather than be dictated by well-connected interest groups or even less technically informed but well-meaning humanitarians. The assumption is that ethical values relative to medicine are different from those for national infrastructure building. Stated more simply, one size does not fit all, and no man or woman or organization has the experience and understanding to judge ethics for everybody. But everybody needs ethical standards. Allowing standards to emerge organically in real-time is dealing with the problem before the politics and ideology fog sets in.

3. NGOs tend to effectively use persuasion in dealing with an erring membership, which is always preferable to government policing.

The next logical question is what to measure to keep artificial intelligence in human hands and ensure that the technology remains in the right human hands? One can hope that supporters and donors widely agree on a given metric and make it openly accessible and verifiable.

Table 8.2: *NGO Measurement Attributes*

Attribute	Pay Attention to
Ethics- specific	Conscience, shared wisdom, fairness, robustness, safety, accountability, calling, beneficence, explainability, data monopoly, sustainability are human values to consider.
Sector-specific	Ethics in energy, health, materials, industrials, consumer discretionary, consumer staples, health care, finance, real estate, IT, telecommunication, utilities, biology, and others have unique needs not shared by other sectors, and some common ones.

Cause and effect

The term cause-and-effect is often misused and misunderstood. For example, a tabloid reports that teenagers who read at least one book per month tend to wind up in high-paid positions at age 30. Would it be reasonable then to presume that teenage reading causes income to go up later? In this context, can any given ethics regime cause good things to happen, or can an ethics regime prevent bad things from happening? The answer is a decisive yes and no.

> Every day we observe relationships between a set of factors called causes and a resulting phenomenon called effect. If (A) causes (B), then we know that (A) must exist, and it must come first. Even a categorical statement that says smoking causes cancer is not entirely accurate because people who do not smoke can get cancer as well. In contrast, some people who do smoke never get cancer. To get around that logic, we use probability. Cause (A) has a high likelihood but does not necessarily cause an effect (B). The measurement is a statistical correlation. If the correlation coefficient "r," which ranges from +1 to -1, is close to +1, then a correlation exists. . Correlations only describe the probability, never the cause itself.
>
> The expression "necessary condition" means that if (A) is defined as early age reading and is a necessary cause of (B) defined as a

high-income job at age 30, then the presence of (B) a management job implies the presence of (A) early reading has taken place. The presence of (A), defined as early reading, does not imply that (B), a management job, will follow later.

The mathematics of Cause-and-Effect applied to ethics can become more complicated in physics, biology, medicine, and psychology.

For purposes of getting an ethics discussion explored in a group setting, a closer look at the so-called Cause & Effect Fishbone Diagram is helpful. The Diagram is a tool for a group of management people to stay focused. The technique is attributed to a Japanese business scholar by the name of Ishikawa. Toyota, the automobile company, first applied a quality management program called Six Sigma to identify quality problems after an observed effect without a reasonable explanation. Borrowing this approach and using it to technology's ethics issues is one way to deal with the situation. For example, if it turns out that an algorithm shows a bias, was the tendency learned, programmed, how did it happen, what good or bad does it do, who benefits, and does it violate existing laws or ethics rules? The following example assumes a right to be forgotten as in the European Union. It also assumes that a right to be remembered does not exist.

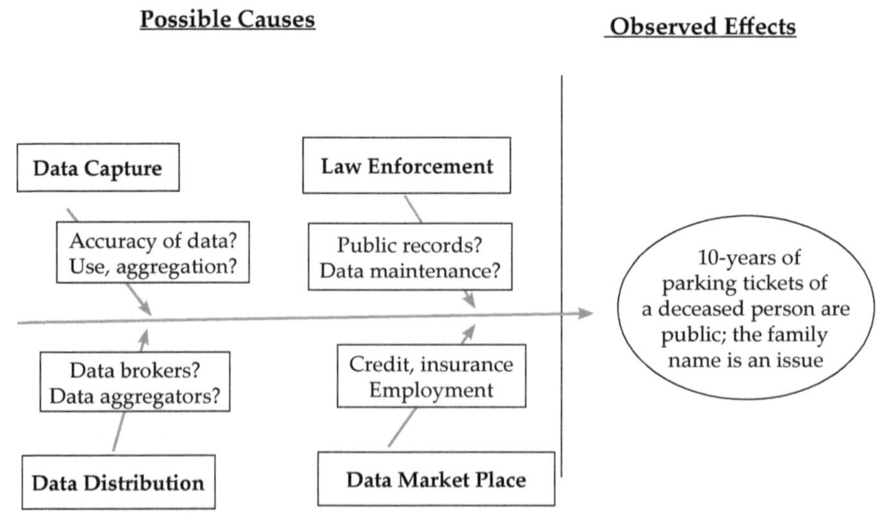

Figure 8.1: *Cause and Effect Diagram applied to the ethics Right to be Forgotten.*

The above diagram is a cause-and-effect framework for a hypothetical situation where a deceased person with a famous name from a small town has unpaid parking tickets on record. Family members and many persons with remarkably similar names have filed a complaint under an ordinance called "The Right to be Forgotten." The diagram is the discussion framework for an ethics panel to find a solution to correct the issue and prevent similar problems from coming up in the future. The law enforcement departments of municipalities are the most likely beneficiary of this approach. In addition, litigators for the claimants would also benefit because the resolution involves a fee. An ethics panel, in this case, need not always be composed of high-priced specialists.

While the Right to be Forgotten for the individual John Q. Public seems small, the issue is significant when it applies to many John Q. Publics on a national scale. Some people suffer from the easy availability of personal files and their manipulation; even data value diminishes over time. What is right and what is wrong is also a function of culture. The lack of clarity often is the excuse for not being able to establish rules. For example, the moral issue of meeting an obligation to the community, like food standards, applies to every corporation. Theoretically, all rights under the law should be examined concerning Artificial Intelligence technologies and appropriately interpreted. That is a considerable task with unknown outcomes. Firms have to develop thought-through answers for their general questions, and the Cause-and-Effect Diagram can help.

The diagram's original purpose was error detection- and correction to improve the quality of Toyota automobiles, a purpose it served par excellence. It is safe to assume that algorithms mimicking humans make mistakes just like humans do, sometimes the same ones.

Indexing

Would it not be convenient to have an index number for most ethics cases for any industry? Insert the parameters and hit a GO button? And if the number $\geq Z$, then and all is well? No more questions to ask; we are done. No ethics committee to argue with, no lawsuits to challenge us, and above all, no human rights violated. However, if a lack of trust in artificial intelligence is the issue, then an ethics index is unlikely to change that situation. Conventionally, an index is a formula expressing a relationship between one dimension to another dimension. A start point for an index is usually 100. Indices are constructed, invented, and redefined to fit a given need at the time. The closest thing to an ethics index comes from an annual United Nations (UNDP) report called HDI, which stands for Human Development Index. That particular index measures three dimensions globally: human reproductive health, empowerment, and labor market participation. It tracks nations from year to year concerning progress along those lines. Out of 189 countries, Norway ranks as # 1 and as US #17. While this metric touches on ethics and qualifies as an index, anything like this may not be well suited for measuring Artificial Intelligence's ethics.

Sustainability as a moral obligation – The case for the Triple Bottom Line

Advocates of climate change and waste reductions render admirable services to society, but they cannot claim any intellectual property right for inventing the concept of sustainability. The term comes from the Latin word *sustinere,* meaning to hold. Since the beginning of forestry- management in the late 1800s in the United States, sustainability has become a genuinely ethical management concept and a role model for everything since then. George Vanderbilt established the Biltmore estate in Asheville, North Carolina, and employed Dr. Carl Schenk from Germany to build the first forestry school. Ironically, the need for responsible management of a natural resource became apparent only after the forests of Western North Carolina were clearcut to export lumber and make tar to waterproof wooden ships. The goal was to make money, and the lessons for today are apparent!

Do we have to wait for current Artificial Intelligence technologies to sacrifice our values to feed the finance industry in the hope for another Dr. Schenk-equivalent 100 years from now? The forestry concept goes under the name of "sustained yield." To explain, just picture a managed area of land with lots of trees growing on it. The rate of tree growth of the entire forest easily translates into cubic feet of lumber per year. Under a sustained yield strategy, the annual capacity of the lumber mill to cut lumber equals the tree growth rate on the land on which it sits. Thus, our hypothetical lumber mill can operate forever, except for the probability of an occasional forest fire. The technology of mathematical optimization now makes the

Western North Carolina forests sustainable to feeding paper mills. That means trees cannot reach maturity as young trees grow fiber faster than older trees do. Fiber content is the objective. Human nature has remained the same, it appears.

A valuable lesson for crafting near future ethics rules is treating human nature as a constant, not a variable.

The modern use of the word "sustainability" still embraces the central "operating forever" idea. Here is a bit of contemporary history: In 1972, The Club of Rome published *The Limits of Growth* report. The Club is a global think tank headquartered in Winterthur, Switzerland. The report addressed worldwide resource constraints linked to growth and succeeded in getting worldwide attention. Fifteen years later, the United Nations published *Our Common Future,* also known as the "Brundtland Report." It defines sustainability, paraphrased here, as *meeting the needs of our current* generation, *but not at the expense of the next generation.* Gro Harlem Brundtland was a former Norwegian prime minister commissioned by the United Nations to work on sustainable development issues. In 1992, the United Nations organized the Earth Summit conference in Rio de Janeiro, resulting in "Agenda 21," a blueprint for global sustainable development. Next in the line of progress was The Kyoto Agreement (1997), which focused on carbon emission to alleviate global warming concerns. The Kyoto Agreement instituted carbon pollution trading for companies as a way to incentivize worldwide sustainability.

New problems call for new metrics with increasing urgency! The *Triple Bottom Line* is an accounting framework to address money, the environment, and humans. It is of relatively recent origin, 1994.

Table 8.3: *Triple Bottom Line Accounting Framework*

Domain	*Purpose*	*Benchmark in Year$_0$ Actual Value*	*Measurement1*	*Measurement2*
Profit	Solvency	Current ratio current (assets/liabilities)	%change from Last year,+	%change From Year$_0$
	Profit	Net profit margin Net (income/operating revenue	%change from Last year, +	%change From Year$_0$
	Leverage	Debt ratio Total debt/total assets	%change from Last year, -	%change From Year$_0$
	Market value	PE ratio Price per share/earnings	%change from Last year, +	%change From Year$_0$
	Growth	Δ S(sales) = $S_s - S_0$	%change from Last year, +	%change From Year$_0$
People	wages	Lowest annual wage as a percent of the official poverty level	%change from Last year, +	%change From Year$_0$
	Health	Percent of full and part-time Employees covered by insurance	%change from Last year, +	%change From Year$_0$
	Learning	Corporate training expenses, incl. Tuition refund, as a % of revenue	%change from Last year, +	%change From Year$_0$
	Equity	Highest annual employee personal total income, as a % of lowest	%change from Last year, -	%change From Year$_0$
	Society	Financial support for non-PAC community projects, % of net profit	%change from Last year, +	%change From Year$_0$
Planet	CO_2	Tons emitted in operations	%change from Last year, -	%change From Year$_0$
	H_2O	Gal/year water used in operations	%change from Last year +	%change From Year$_0$
	Energy	Σ(kwh}, fleet gasoline, diesel, heating oil, coal, used, in BTUs	%change from Last year, -	%change From Year$_0$
	Remediation, Dumpsite clean-up, wetland restoring	Investments in alternative energy count for carbon neutrality, estimate BTU value, as % of current use, land-use	%change from Last year, +	%change From Year$_0$

F. Wolf, *Measurements*, Bookboon,

Folk wisdom in the art of measurement

> ***Please tell me how you will measure me, and I will tell you how I will behave.***
>
> **Eli Goldratt**

Successful measurement is both art and science, and rules and methods that evolve from practice must be paid attention to; in fact, books on crowd wisdom are in print.

Goldratt was an Israeli physicist who made a bit of a name for himself with a management protocol called the Theory of Constraint. That theory, so-called, recognizes that all managers work to overcome limitations. Overcoming constraints starts with identifying the constraining condition itself, exploiting it if possible, followed by synchronization and elevating the rule, and repeating the process ad infinitum. Once a given constraint is under control, there will always be a new one on the horizon. While the theory itself is not the critical point here, it supports the timeless idea of continuous improvement, which was also part of the quality movement in the business many years earlier. The quality movement started after WWII when it became apparent that Japanese products ranked higher than their US competitors' products. The quality of products and services was the strategic focus for Japan Inc. In the present quest for better ethics in Artificial Intelligence; the takeaway is that industry is unlikely to reach a perfect state of ethics, and any enterprise must continuously seek ethical improvements. Ethics is not a single number. Goldratt's behavioral insight suggests that humans may respond to incentives based on sound ethical outcomes.

> ***Our deepest fear is not inadequacy; our deepest fear is that we are powerful beyond measure.***
>
> **Marianne Williamson**

Marianne Williamson, a successful author, is credited with the above quote. In the instant context of artificial intelligence, who could be "powerful beyond all measure" and exert a disproportionate influence? About five or more major US and international technology firms come to mind. Those firms share the common denominators of making more money than large nations have in tax income. Money translates into power, and power corrupts, while absolute power corrupts absolutely. (Lord Acton, 1834 – 1902). No growth is not an option for those companies. A corporation founded on idealism is not guaranteed to stay on that path.

Doing what you like is freedom;
liking what you do is happiness.
Frank Tyger

In chapter 1, John Stuart Mills' Utilitarianism came up as a potential moral guidepost for artificial intelligence. In particular, the idea of the greatest happiness. Tyger was a cartoonist and editor for a newspaper in New Jersey and coined the catchy phrase quoted above. It is safe to assume that ethics is measurable and that applied to artificial intelligence is equally measurable. Happiness, or human well-being, is a goal for this new technology, and it is hard to define. Human happiness has a different meaning than satisfying every human want. It is undoubtedly an arduous undertaking to quantify happiness or even mere contentment. On the other hand, giving up on delaying measuring ethics is tantamount to inviting bad outcomes by neglect.

In business, there is a natural tension between profit and ethics. The technology of Artificial Intelligence is not an exception. We want the technology to assist us in making more money but not limit our authority over the technology that helps us. It would be an error to presume that firms are as idealistic now as they were initially. If the income generated from carbon trading lowers the probability of our planet's overheating, that is one good thing. Well-defined and honest metrics for artificial intelligence do not exist yet. One can assume for the moment that the European Unions' GDPR is a leading indicator of what is to come in the US and elsewhere. Private sector collaboration with regulators is a necessity, and the sooner, the better!

CHAPTER 9
THE NEXT LEVEL – QUANTUM COMPUTING

Given the long patterns of past technology waves to get established, one may expect that the Artificial Intelligence wave has just arrived, while the brunt of it is still to come. On the other hand, Quantum Computing is not quite here yet, but may be soon based on funding and interest in the subject. Quantum computing represents a subset of Artificial Intelligence and a particular ethics case. Classical computing is ethically similar to quantum computing, except that the latter is fast. Classical computing has not changed much in the last five decades. Computing has become a lot faster, but still is a function of human inputs into a box. With speed comes the ability to do both good and evil even better.

The same observations hold for classical algorithms that begin to run our digital lives soon to be more powerful in terms of positive and negative characteristics. On the negative side, a quantum-empowered Intelligence will advance what we fear most, namely the fear of losing control over technology. Consider the current military illustration of the detectability of conventional missiles and subsequent destruction. Then consider hypersonic missiles that are not detectable in time. Perhaps a remedy for hypersonic missiles is that eventually, a solution will become available. The world does not stand still. The connection between quantum computing, which is the enormous power to process data into information, and Artificial Intelligence, which is human-like thinking of machines aided by super-fast computing, requires new rules of conduct for humans themselves. Getting there in an orderly manner is possible via initial self-regulation and subsequent government intervention in the commercial sector. Governments on which we rely to enforce commerce standards have also weaponized quantum computing for economic- and military defense and even for economic aggression.

Quantum

The "big Q" started when the German physicist Max Planck (1858 – 1947) discovered that energy comes in the form of packets, which he called "quanta," where a so-called *"quanta"* is the radiation frequency multiplied by a constant value. That numeric constant is similar in mathematics, as is the value of pi (π), 3.14, the ratio of the circumference of a circle to its radius. Another comparison is the value "C" in Einstein's famous $E = MC^2$. Here the constant C represents the theoretical speed of light. Planck's quanta number is 6.62607015 X 10^{-34} joules/ second. Planck received the Nobel Laureate in 1919 on this small number, which is now the core of Quantum Theory.

A branch of modern mathematics is Quantum Mechanics. It enables a way to describe energy packets' behavior at the sub-atomic level, like electrons spinning around neutrons in strange ways. Those tiny electrons can become entangled with each other, and they can also appear in two places simultaneously, all of which goes under the term "quantum weirdness." The word *"mechanics"* in "Quantum Mechanics" refers to the *mechanica*l ways of quantifying electrons' behavior. Quantum computing may eventually extend Moore's Law claiming that the number of transistors on a microchip doubles every two years, and the cost of computers halves simultaneously. With quantum computing, Moore's Law may have a new lease on life, even though quantum computing is not digital and therefore does not depend on transistors. Quantum calculations are achieved with entangled particles and designed to increase computing capacity at a double exponential rate, which is amazingly fast. Mathematically, if "exponential" is defined as $(N)^2$, then double exponential is $((N)^2)^2$. In traditional and digital computing, a "bit" is the lowest element of information, and it can be either *on* or *off* as shown in the binary code below:

binary code in bits	2^0	2^1	2^2	2^3 …
decimals equivalent	1	2	4	8
binary (8+1) is decimal 9	1	0	0	1

In quantum computing, the bit-equivalent is called a "qubit." A qubit can be in at least three states at the same time. as shown below:

state | zero >: (1/0)

state | one >: (0/1)

state | both >: (1/1)

So far, all solvable problems on a traditional computer are equally solvable on a quantum computer and the other way around. Theoretically, there is no advantage in quantum computing over classical computing other than time. Consider computability! The digital software that runs our society now cannot operate on quantum computers! Conventional software manipulates bits; it cannot manipulate qubits. The fundamental difference between quantum computers over their classical cousins lies in its speed to finish a routine. If programable quantum computers solve a problem that traditional computers cannot now solve in any (reasonable) amount of time, then (Ψ), or the state of quantum supremacy, has been reached.

Trying to imagine a sub-atomic world where electrons can be entangled and be in two different places simultaneously is difficult for human observers living in the visual world to believe. Is reality really real, or just "artificial" like new forms of intelligence nowadays? Edwin Schrödinger (1887 – 1961) tried to explain that paradox to Einstein at Yale University in 1935. Einstein did not buy that argument. That thought experiment is now known as Schrödinger's Cat.

Interest in Artificial Intelligence technologies became a priority after it became evident that computing machines could improve human decision-making. That was around 1956 when the Dartmouth conference convened to establish Artificial Intelligence as a discipline. By the time 1980 rolled around, Expert Systems began to aid humans in managing their problems. Currently, computers have narrowly exceeded the human ability to solve the game of GO, for example. That was impressive, but not earthshaking. The power of average human brains to think, reason, and compute remains the benchmark for new technologies. Mathematically, the ill-understood capacity of the human brain qualifies as only the lowest common denominator, for the moment. Although the term "benchmark" sounds better. Before we fear the coming of a runaway ethic resulting from Quantum Computing, let us remember that even quantum computers lack emotions, self-awareness, value.

Information ethics

Within the rubric of Information Ethics, starting about two decades or more ago, is a body of literature dealing with librarianship and electronic data processing. Again, the word *ethics* comes from the Greek "ethos" and means "good." Philosophy separates good from not-so-good based on morality. Good- and bad principles apply equally to quantum computing as they do to Information Ethics. Ethical concerns range from privacy to property, accuracy, and access. The GDPR- and the State of California already deal with those concerns and even enforce them. For instance, it matters who controls data, who receives it, who manages and owns the story.

Creating data is a path to power and money, lots of both. Combining multiple pieces of information from numerous sources does create new knowledge. The famous phrase that "*data is the new oil*" comes to mind. Making money is not evil; even Adam Smith said so by pointing to the evidence of the "invisible hand." Power by itself is not wrong either, even though "power corrupts, and absolute power corrupts absolutely," according to Lord Acton (1834 – 1902). The best of intentions may sometimes end badly. Bad outcomes can result from human error or deceitful intent. Companies like Google, Amazon, Wal-Mart, and Apple, to name the well-knowns, are engaged in beneficial and legal data harvesting. But when such data are sold and combined with other data, moral dilemmas can arise anywhere in the information chain. Quantum computing will contribute to this problem by creating new information with more significant uncertainty and faster than ever before. Succeeding in the sciences of quantum computing requires considerable skill and a heavy concentration of investments, plus distribution capabilities that are only available to the few. When skills, assets, and distribution are in the hands of a few operators, it naturally leads to a data monopoly with moral consequences. Competition is good, but monopoly, defined as the ability to set prices, is not.

Dissemination of data refers to the release of data from one source to another and their combination and permutation. Data originating from government sources like various censuses and the financial sector are reasonably well regulated and beneficial and, in fact, necessary. University- and industry-based scientific sources generally observe ethical rules. Private funding intended to influence scientific conclusions is a developing ethics dilemma enabled by quantum computing. On the other hand, quantum computing may create value by double-checking for fake findings. In the absence of clarity, one can always start with trust in initial self-regulation.

Ownership of data, especially by the company which created such data, is a right. Its use, even if it leads to a commercial monopoly, is legal and moral. The argument that humans catatonically own their profile information is not a good one because people provide it free in exchange for free services. In the case of a company/website called *ancestry.com*, the company owns outright their customers' DNA. Again, if customers do not care one way or another, there is no real ethical problem because data is made freely available under clearly understood conditions. Ownership can morph into censorship! The actors to watch out for are the ordinary cast of commercial operators and governments, particularly those governments around the world suspected to fudge elections.

The organization of data is any activity of classifying and organizing information to increase its utility. Future designs will have to embrace the effects of both Artificial Intelligence and quantum computing. The practice of labeling images by the millions of workers in low-wage countries for machines to learn from is one such classifying activity. The moral question of who will benefit and who will be disadvantaged remains to be answered.

Quantum computing ethics

Quantum computing and Artificial Intelligence are moral, and in quantum-speak, entangled.

Quantum computing, as mentioned earlier, takes place in qubits which can be in more than one state (on, off, or both, at any one time. In traditional computing, bits are either on or off, and the states are in are those of their registers. When a qubit triggers an action, its initial state is not known. Its output is therefore only probable. That fact introduces a new level of uncertainty solely due to quantum computing. Another issue is that software written for digital computers does not run on quantum computers. That means recoding all digital software for quantum computers is necessary. When debugging quantum software, the actual state of the initial qubits will remain unknown because making a copy of a quantum object and inspecting one is not possible in this technology. Even Schrödinger could not physically see his second cat, although he certainly *knew* it was there.

Ethically, quantum computing and Artificial Intelligence are in similar boats. Quantum computing needs to develop standards under which outputs can be deemed reliable, and Artificial Intelligence needs criteria under which its decisions can be considered trustworthy. Yet, it is reasonable, for example, to foresee quantum encryption to be declared a secure communication environment at some future point in time by providers of quantum computing, most likely.

Neither Artificial Intelligence nor quantum computing is by itself wrong. Still, applications may lead to situations that make those technologies appear less correct. You guessed it; the remedy is a combination of self-regulation, co-regulation, legislation, and advocacy enforcement for the Good in these technologies. Trust comes first, clarity soon after that.

What is required	trust in data and computing
What is forbidden	stealing money, especially from bitcoins, price fixing, ransom software, fudging elections etc.

Quantum computing applications

Cryptography is the basis for nearly all secure communications relative to financial data and medical data, for instance. Cryptography is the art of coding information for only receivers and senders to understand. That principle goes back to biblical times when Hebrews and Ephraimites pronounced the word "shibboleth" differently and became identifiable as either friend or foe. In WWII, the German Enigma machine transmitted secure military information until Poland decrypted that code, followed by France and England. A 2012 television series called "The Bletchley Girls" describes the English efforts to break the Enigma encryption code in which Alan Turing, of Artificial Intelligence fame, had a significant hand.

Modern encryption methods use integer factorization. For example, the number is 32 created from (8) times (4). The number 8 in turns factors from (2)(2)(2). It turns out that the number 4 factors into (2)(2). Thus, breaking a 250-digit code number into its lowest possible prime number was not even thinkable until not too long ago when quantum computing entered the scene.

Anything that encrypts can also, sooner or later, be decrypted!

The ability of hackers to intercept secure communications becomes dangerous as soon as hackers can also break access codes. Quantum computing may play a role in breaking codes as well as making new ones. The cat-and-mouse game is likely to continue.

Quantum Search of databases will be possible once quantum computing becomes operational. What is modestly called a "quantum supremacy" state will have been reached once quantum search becomes a lot faster than classical search. This condition may or may not raise immediate ethical concerns. However, a future quantum algorithm may iterate through all possible combinations in a database search by guessing the access codes to files and gain unauthorized access. Quantum computing, in this case, could be complicit in the theft of information, which is a very lucrative business but ethically and legally forbidden. Assume the worst first.

Financial modeling has evolved into science by itself, but unlike modeling in physical sciences in which nature is the constraint, there are no controlled settings for monetary experimentation. Investors often wish to evaluate many probable outcomes in which quantum computing may help, especially in arbitrage. Ethics concerns are never far from financial considerations! After all, the goal of investing is to make money. Quantum computing certainly adds to the number of investment options one can consider in a reasonable time frame.

But on the other hand, it also increases uncertainty as sampling errors pile on quantum computing errors. Ethics in financial modeling should first start with human intent. A return on investment is undoubtedly all right, and so is arbitrage. However, hiding known risks is off-limits.

Weather Forecasting affects $6 trillion in US food production, according to National Oceanic and Atmospheric Administration (NOAA). Local weather forecasting is often inaccurate because the weather moves faster than it takes to collect data. Quantum computing will make weather forecasting more accurate for smaller geographies.

CHAPTER 10
REGULATORY CHALLENGES

In practice, business life is different from the prescriptions offered by the average technology magazine claiming to have the answers. Those answers usually suggest that *all* corporations *must* do this or do that, and all will be well if they do. The missing link is who is responsible for achieving a workable regulatory environment for this technology? Much of the nitty-gritty day-to-day challenges fall on corporate compliance departments and the CEOs who supervise them. Strong is good, and weak is terrible. Whether society controls ethics in Artificial Intelligence technologies by self-regulation, legislation, or a combination of both, the very act of regulating will present challenges. Enforcement is only one of these challenges. The discussion that follows is industry neutral. That means stated principles apply to many industrial sectors equally, and the difficulties listed are not exhaustive. This chapter considers algorithm model risks, data governance, customers' privacy, supervisors' supervision, and administration. In the early days of the Internet, the hype message was that the Internet is an excellent mechanism for democratizing information. Everybody on the planet will have affordable access to everything, and all of humankind is thereby bound to flourish. The dark side of Artificial Intelligence now is the preferred tool for dictators to undo democracy by sabotaging elections, opportunists to steal money and intellectual property. The regulatory challenge is to enable the Good in Artificial Intelligence to emerge and to prevail.

Model Risk

Risks are present in nearly all algorithms. Every enterprise runs models that include rule-based algorithms to make predictions or decisions. Integrity demands that model responses are reviewed and updated and never, ever, 100% entrusted to a machine. The updating function is the model operators' responsibility. That responsibility includes, at minimum, model integrity and moral principles like not to harm. If a given model is a simulation, it should explain plausible outcomes by stating which variables changed and how they changed. Consequential algorithms have to be stress-tested for humans to understand the plausibility of results. All companies must inventory all operational models and review their performance in timely intervals, whether operating under self-regulation or legislated rules. That, unfortunately, is unlikely to be the case all the time. Before older models replace newer ones, both old and new have to run parallel before an old version officially expires. Continuously monitoring every operational algorithm is an ethical imperative to identify false negatives and false positives. To be fully aware of this critical mandate, think of model risk in the fields of medicine, aviation, credit, or that of elections.

In summary, achieving a modicum of ethics is much work. It will cost money, which, when properly accounted for, can offset some productivity gains on the other side of the ledger. Not talking about this and hoping that the problem will quietly disappear is an attractive and low-cost option for mediocre management.

Data Governance and Bias

Data is the vital spark that makes Artificial Intelligence come alive, as the technology's appetite for data is ravenous. When newly generated information serves its purpose, people will have gained helpful insights because the data was quality and sufficient. Otherwise, the figure of speech from the early days of data processing is GIGO (garbage in – garbage out).

Rules for data ethics often come in vague language. There is one exception: "First, do no harm.", (*primum non nocere*). That rule comes from Hippocrates (460-375 BC). In the field of mathematical statistics, vagueness happens in sampling theory. For example, a medication may be approved based on being 95% effective, which means that the odds of not working is 5:100. The most misleading data error is to infer a cause from a correlation. Misleading popular phrases are "help prevent" or "helps promote," followed by a condition that may apply. Misleading a client with half-truths is just a little bit unethical but certainly not illegal.

In current practice, self-regulating organizations like FINRA and ISO impose ethics-like rules upon their very substantial memberships. In the FINRA case, rule enforcement is transparent: violate our SEC-approved trading regulations, and you can't trade securities; an existential issue for brokers/dealers, the nuclear option. In the ISO case, violate our product- or service quality standards, and you cannot use our 9000- or 14000- designation that infers value for your business. Governments impose standards through the courts or police departments. The General Data Protection Regulation (GDPR), a law in the European Union and not an organization, now enforces its rules with court-approved fines. While the GDPR rules are motivated by ethics, those rules also apply to nations outside the European Union competing inside. Politics and money also tend to weaken ethics on the national level.

All data is biased, even the local weather report, when potential danger is over-reported. According to the popular press, bias is terrible because it favors something over something else and maybe disadvantageous to someone along that path. Accepting those statements for a moment, how can anything be good when everything is biased when bias per se is bad? Accepting some form of discrimination as an existing condition is realistic. Suppose we start with a rule of not harming and conducting our business with high commercial honor; we now have a starting point to advance from. FINRA members are obliged to operate with a "high commercial honor." If that seems complicated to define in every instance, the absence of high commercial honor becomes apparent when presented with the facts. A machine-learned (ML) system about college admission may repeat past biases in subtle ways. For instance, private college admission data may show a preference for admitting the children of alumni. That may be all right on the basis that the institution is private. But if the student body exceeds 50,000, is it still private enough to have those rules?

If we define "bias" as unfairly favoring one thing over another, we still have to determine what those "things" are. In the context of technology, some "things" are in chapter 4. Is it safe, is it harmful, or even helpful? There are four practical steps along the path of eliminating detrimental biases at the corporate level.

Step 1 is to review all corporate data sources used in all models for potential bias. Under normal circumstances, the people who build models do that, but a more diverse group from Finance, Operations, and Customer Services need to render ethical decisions. Diversity alone would not guarantee fairness. Training to perform such evaluations is necessary in most cases to assure a good result. To do such a review once a year may be sufficient.

Step 2 is to verify all data sources in operating models, at regular intervals, for detrimental changes that may have occurred over time. Data may come from open-source libraries; data may come from so-called aggregators who create data, and from from social media, which is always a moving target, and data that can internally generate data. Should data changes over time lead to unreliability, it may influence management decisions.

Step 3, to evaluate any possible integration of data. In the not-so-distant past, data used to reside in so-called data silos. Here each corporate department guarded its very own data for its use and interpretation. The modern approach is to create so-called data- lakes. Data- lakes tend to store data in its raw format for corporate customers to apply as needed. Raw data tends to be more accurate than data that is already processed. The raw data form allows more flexibility in using data.

Step 4 is to assure secure access to data for only those who need to know. Secure access means more than encryption and password schemes and elaborate hacking prevention. For example, secure access now has to shield the data owners from closing down their operations in return for ransom payments.

Data Security and Privacy

Data security is a significant component of data governance. Ethically, data security addresses an existing evil that is beyond the rule of *first do no harm.* For corporate data security, all stakeholders and all supply chain members find themselves in the same boat. Generally, data security means control of access, encryption, and quality checks. In a supply chain, information is, by necessity, shared among many partners. The sharing of data makes supply chains so effective, and it is also the sharing of data that makes supply chains risky. The data security in a supply chain is as good as its weakest connection. One ethics question is whether a given database lends itself to identifying persons and whether personal data is snoop-proof. Corporations have many departments and also have to present a unified security regime to the public. A suitable security approach may dictate a cross-functional information technology governance inside a company and an overall plan-B if something goes wrong. Applications in Artificial Intelligence pull in data from many sources, each posing a new cybersecurity threat. Third-party software vendors are only one of many such opportunities, and virtual assistants are another.

To make a long story short, data's voluntary but self-interest-motivated governance must occur at the corporation level. To do data security well will require a sizeable new workforce with new skills to accomplish. Forensic accounting – and coding are among those skill sets. The new technologies reduce the number of production jobs and, at the same time, increase employment elsewhere. This potential scenario sounds like the perfect argument that this industrial revolution will repeat the pattern of previous ones. Namely, some jobs will be lost and never come back. Other jobs in more significant numbers will emerge, requiring new skills. Whether the new jobs will balance with the lost ones is not foreseeable. But society's arsenal is not out of options. There is always the option of reducing the 5-day work week to 4-days, the concept of universal basic income, extending State-mandated primary education by two years to include community college equivalents. That would delay the entry point of young people into the workforce.

Administration and Outsourcing

The mental images the words "Artificial Intelligence" create is one of the young geniuses in white lab coats manipulating quantum machines to cure all future ills that may befall humanity. The mundane corporate functions like payrolls, benefits administration, operations, inventory control, and paying taxes are not at the forefront. Yet, those are the functions on which Artificial Intelligence thrives because such processes are repetitive and of high volume. Administrative functions are not profit centers and are not in the limelight. The applications in the spotlight are often in the laboratory and may, or may not, bear fruit. Cost reductions achieved via automation affect productivity (output/input). They may easily lead to the improved valuation of securities, which affects the financial security of pensioners, who can subsequently go out to restaurants and support the retail sector. What matters greatly are simple administrative improvements in order processing, searching for documents by keywords, extracting content from legal documents, signature confirmations, invoice reconciliations, detecting anomalies and potential fraud, making predictions, and learning aspects of Artificial Intelligence. Ethics issues are lurking everywhere and are just around the corner. For example, to what extent is this new technology used to control employees in the workplace? Are their health records secure, are their movements continually watched, are their laptops snooped on, exits and entries into facilities recorded, and what about the privacy of their faces? Also, to what extent do corporations have a right and a need to protect themselves from malcontent workers? Should the labor laws of "employment at will" be adjusted to conform to the remote and gig work climate?

Outsourcing introduces a new level of risk. In former times, business strategies aimed for self-sufficiency in everything. Old factories had multiple floors near a river or a railroad line and stretched a large area. The modern business strategy calls for control of only the core technology and outsourcing everything else to reduce duplication and waste. With outsourcing comes the burden of many more hands and eyes on company data, which is a huge security risk for every firm in a supply chain, not just the core brand. Many firms find themselves part of many chains. The irony is that intentional- or unethical use of data along the supply chain can affect the reputation of the company whose name is on the end product if something goes wrong, like forced labor in a remote area of the world.

No regulation for Artificial Intelligence technologies is probably not an option. Better designed- and earlier implemented code emanating from practical experiences is possible!

CHAPTER 11
REGULATORY TRENDS

Artificial Intelligence is tied-up in computing. In this book, Artificial Intelligence and how to keep it under human control is the open question. Computing in this case plays an important, but secondary role because it is the number-crunching aspect of Artificial Intelligence. Consider that here the tail may also be wagging the dog. Coming changes in computing may soon control Artificial Intellilgence, the technology. What appears to be less important may be more important than is currently realized. Traditionally computers are considered boxes into which information is fed, a logic function inside the box takes place, and on the other end of the box the results are presented for the human operator to read and decide. The basic model of input – box – output is still there. That model is now everywhere; it is in our hearing aids, in our cars, cell-phones, in the door that reads your retina to open, and peoples' pacemakers to extend thriving human life. Ever increasingly powerful chips that are the inside of the proverbial computer box and are the basis for the continuance of Moore's Law, make that happen. That single chip will soon be replaced by two chips working in tandem.

1. The standard processor

2. The neural engine

The neural engine chip processes learned data to train your devices like cell phone, hearing aids or pacemaker, to function as designed or better. Once this has happened, the range of possible ethical outcomes range from wonderful to terrible. Hypothetically, learning from personal data could lead to a subtle output hints from the box inside, to smoke more cigarettes because doing so infers greater mental engagement, which is good. Ethically, no giant corporation is responsible for any conclusions, and liability is near zero. The consumer we wish to protect may have come full circle only to realize that ultimately, he/she is responsible for personal actions. The consumers may, or may not, have created their own inputs.

Today's commercial world suggests "moving fast and breaking things," a phrase attributed to Facebook's chief Mark Zuckerberg.

Among economists, the "breaking" part refers to creative destruction, which comes from Joseph Schumpeter, who considered change a constructive component of capitalism's ability to renew itself and thereby survive.

On the other extreme, one can only imagine a desirable future state of ethics in Artificial Intelligence drifting towards a middle ground. Assume that the industry through private initiatives commits to doing just no harm and to operate with high commercial honor? While those terms sound fuzzy for the technology to act on, it is a good starting point when applied to persons, companies, and nations. For humanity to benefit from only those two concepts, both the government- and industry sectors have to cooperate rather than compete. Currently, we have EU regulation enforcing a still modest GDPR laws, and in California, we have a somewhat softer CCPA. Elsewhere, Artificial Intelligence technology is either under State control or none at all. The shared global need is to control and promote public trust in technology. Sounding lofty is the correct way to start a trend towards transitioning into the new technology culture. It will take cooperative planning to anticipate the many immoral side-effects like under-employment, marginalized people and those about to be marginalized. Another ethical trend question is whether technology investments always work to benefit people or not? That fear was addressed as early as 1944 at Bretton Woods, resulting in the establishment of the World Bank and its related institutions. This is another example of a relatively private initiative affecting the governance of global issues where the current need to address the ethics of technology.

In most cases, the motivation behind technology investments is ROI (return on investment), but not all projects benefit people. Investments in Artificial Intelligence are in dire need of having ethical components. The prospective positives and negatives must be balanced in the chambers of responsible leaders. Near the end of WWII, a similar concern arose at the Bretton Woods Conference (July 1-22, 1944), where 44 allied nations gathered to design the new financial world order. The fear was that investments would flow only in the highest return direction and leave the poor part of the world destitute. The then mechanism to deal with this issue was creating the International Monetary Fund (IMF) and the IBRD (World Bank). The current fear is that this unregulated technology can leave humans vulnerable to becoming less human. The danger of humans becoming less human now ranks in importance on par with the post-WWII wealth divide. The British development economist John Maynard Keynes was the leading mover and shaker of the Bretton Woods Conference. A Maynard Keynes equivalent is now needed to bring ethics standards to this technology.

A spark to ignite the storm that will establish ethical standards for this technology has yet to happen. The best place for that to happen is in the private sector for no other reason than that is where the money and the incentives are. The term "that is where the money is" refers to the famous bank robber Willey Sutton. When asked why he is robbing banks, he gave that answer. An estimate of US Artificial Intelligence spending in 2020 is:

Military sector	US$ 4bn	(US Budget)
Public Sector	US$ 1bn	(US Budget)
Private Sector	US$ 37-50bn	(Forbes estimate)

Who, or what sector, is best positioned to lead?

For the US, it is the private sector because that is where the money is together with the diversity of applications. In keeping with Artificial Intelligence's traditions, an academic/industry group not unlike Dartmouth's Summer Research Project of 1956 is a process role model to get started. Such a group could set self-regulation into motion in one industrial sector, followed by many other industrial sectors, and then move forward to embrace more industries. The International Telecommunication Union (ITU) is part of the United Nations family and may lend moral authority to the effort. The UN Charter is broad enough to influence moral standards for its 193 member nations. IEEE and ITU are candidates to take on the leadership vacuum. To the UN's credit, it passed the Law of the Sea, a regulation that most countries observe. But we live in a time when a few giant technology firms, mainly in the US and Communist China, have more money than nations have, and thereby more power, and are now challenging their governments for control. The man on the street is just an innocent bystander.

Trending on what issues to regulate

In the larger scheme of things, " we the people" want to remain in control of our destiny to the extent that is still possible. Under no circumstances are humans to relinquish themselves to a mechanical process like becoming victim of economic optimization. However, a human-machine symbiosis is a good and worthwhile goal. Under a symbiotic philosophy, machine productivity increases to benefit people, and the economy aligns with a social contract of not creating a new class of victims. In such an enforceable arrangement, green investments may flourish without governmental subsidies. A trend for ethical questions to be addresses is going to touch all of us in the following ways:

Privacy v technology

For technology to effect change, people may have to let go of a few sacred cows. How much is an individual choice and the regulators' choice? Experience has shown that individuals are pretty liberal with trading private data for convenience. Think of any Facebook profile. Anybody who reveals personal feelings to thousands of Facebook friends has no argument to object to a Census question on the grounds of privacy.

Sovereignty v globalization

Successful globalization presumes a peaceful integration of global markets and global companies. Globalization may have reached its peak as authoritarian governments embrace nationalism over globalization. Globalization quietly tramples on cultural values like speech, diet, dress, music and more. Think of Bitcoins vs. the sovereignty of national currencies controlled by central banks.

Elites v ordinary people

Elites and commoners have existed since the beginning of time and may forever more. The measurement for this is usually wealth or access to assets combined with influence. That is natural because no human is exactly like any another human. Artificial Intelligence can both help reduce and increase the gap in status; but its elimination is not even an objective. Communists tried to close the rich-poor gap by the 1917 revolution and succeeded only in creating a different class of privilege.

Optimization v caring

Optimizations conjure up an image of cold-hearted mathematical logic sans any human considerations. While that can be so in some business cases, in practice it not always is. For example, optimizing resource allocations in the paper industry called for mathematical programming with constraint equations that guaranteed all loggers a livelihood. Only after that was done, did the cold logic begin. Many current research papers in Artificial Intelligence ethics point to the trend of programming ethics into algorithms. Mathematically, optimizations can accommodate ethical constraints, but let us watch out for who writes the programs. The dangerous trend is to build ethics agents into autonomous systems. Machines can be programmed, and they can always learn to perform tasks that are learned from continuous data. Machines do learn, but they don't understand.

On a global scale the trends are for the positives of AI to far outweigh the negatives of AI. Therefore, everybody is excited to move forward with Artificial Intelligence. But could unemployment in some corners of the world become so massive as a result of machines becoming smarter, as to affect societal balances? Or could a technology-based civil unrest become widespread while governments run out of money- printing options? Or could a handful of global technology firms become richer than entire countries and decide not to follow the rules any longer? Or could military Artificial Intelligence transition into the commercial markets and become accessible to hackers, scammers, anarchists, and similar shady characters? After all, drug cartels already use drones and submarines in their trade. Lastly, and fortunately not a trend yet, could the technology of quantum computing get into the hands of competitors bent on breaking all security codes and thereby produce chaos? Most likely somewhere in the world somebody is working along those lines.

One ethics global trend should be to preserve- and strengthen the middle class, if not all but eliminate most poverty causes. According to Pew Research, a lower-middle family's income in the United

States varies from $32,000 to $53,000 per year, and 68% of Americans self-identify as middle class. The ethical standard to aim for is to improve everybody's lot with this technological opportunity in our time. Previous industrial revolutions have accomplished that more or less coincidentally. Now the governmental policy arsenal to pre-empt massive instability includes:

1. Reduce the standard for full-time jobs to 32 hours/week from 40 hours/week without income loss for jobholders. That sounds hard to do but let us recall that at one point in time, workers had Sunday off to rest and go to church, then came Saturday off as well and two weeks or more of paid vacations after that. As firms benefit from significant productivity gains, a higher unemployment rate may result. One can expect screams of objections to this scheme from many corners. In the 1900's, 40% of the US population lived on farms, while 120 years later, that number is less than 2%, and food is more abundant than ever. At current trends, the rate of change will be much faster.

2. The need to reskill workers for the coming 4th industrial revolution is not in question. Primary education in the US is a State constitutional mandate. Voters and legislators could upscale this mandate to include two-year junior college, rather than limit it to high school. In some instances, this is already happening, and two benefits accrue. One is that young workers will enter the labor pool later, and the other is that they will be better prepared for work-life when they do and earn more income over their lifetime.

3. AI technologies will deliver substantial productivity gains and improvements to human life. At the same time, the technology also makes the less engaged workers more vulnerable to being replaced. The 4th industrial revolution presents an historic opportunity to eliminate many institutionalized indignities of poverty. Technology cannot protect all people from all wounds, but it can ameliorate the hurt. Another approach is called Universal Basic Income; schemes like that are in test phases to eliminate poverty as technology increases the gap between fully employed and under-employed.

The power distance between technology firms and regulators tends to shrink, as the industry gains power, and the government is losing leverage. In democracies that is the trends, while under authoritarian regimes that is the counter-trend. Accepting for a moment that money is power, then the power brokers of the coming 4th Industrial Revolution will significantly influence the regulatory process. Relative to ethics, Silicon Valley elites may prefer to bury the subject rather than help define it to buy time. Case in point: Companies are reaching the dollar weight of nations, and both nations and companies are beginning to act like it too!

2020 revenue of technology firms		v	2017 Budget of nations**	
Amazon	$113 B		Sweden	$271 B
Apple	$274 B		Russia	$258 B
Alphabet (Google)	$182 B		Switzerland	$242 B
Microsoft	$143 B		Argentina	$120 B

** Photins.com

Communist China fired the first such salvo. This conflict is about State v privately owned commercial interest. In western societies, the competition is similar, only the methods of enforcement are different. Jack Ma, the wealthiest person in China and founder of Ant Group and Alibaba, openly criticized the head of State, Xi Jinping, for stifling innovation, among other sins. The modern totalitarian solution is to invite Mr. Ma for a Dutch-Uncle talk. Overnight, the State is "invested" in Mr. Ma's Ant Group, and Alibaba effectively lost control. Mr. Ma is also minus the media fame he loved so much. This intervention places China at the forefront of technology regulation without being a role model.

In the democratic world, similar goals are pursued through the court system to prevent monopolies from forming. A modern alternative, and perhaps a bit unusual perhaps, would offer technology firms an opportunity to engage and sit on the table with co-regulatory status. When the UN was founded, it granted The Holy See and the Federation of the Red Cross and Red Crescent non-voting observer status in the General Assembly. A group of about ten top technology firms may pool their interest into one not-for-profit entity Such an entity may apply for a temporary non-voting United Nations General Assembly membership seat. That would link the technology to ethical norms already part of the UN Charter. The purpose is to have the technology associated with a worldwide moral framework, at least in appearance. It is distinctly possible that a good appearance can lead to a good reality. Technology is trying to define a moral framework for this planet's future. A UN observer status would establish a forum for an ethical technology framework more than global conferences have in the past. Both parties, the United Nations, and the Artificial Intelligence community, would benefit from the association and learn how to accommodate the 4th Industrial Revolution. The first two paragraphs of the United Nations Charter aim to free everybody from the "scourge of war" and reaffirm " fundamental human rights," neither of which has happened so far. On top of that, the nature of "war" now includes cyber wars and other outlets for innate human aggression.

The first step is to petition one or more UN States members to introduce a motion to that effect. Only a nation-state can do that. At this point, Artificial Intelligence technology becomes political. If all the technology giants in the United States, United Kingdom, China, France and Russia combine and each petitioned their governments for one observer seat in the General Assembly, the issue becomes political. The hypothetical outcome, a frenzy to compete on leadership, may have unintended consequence from which the rest of humanity on earth may benefit. Easier to get started along those lines is an Artificial Intelligence non-profit trade group, like the Association for the Advancement of Artificial Intelligence (AAAI) could petition the United Nations for non-governmental organization (NGO) status and start exerting a pro-techno ethics influence.

The subject of ethics in military Artificial Intelligence deserves more consideration. However, it is not news to observe that military technology is both defensive- or aggressive in intent. In the past, benign military technologies were superglue, duct tape, the 4-wheel drive Jeep, and of course, replicas of General MacArthur's sunglasses. A consequential example dates back to 1795 when Napoleon wrote the equivalent of a request for a proposal (RFP) to preserve food for his army on the move into Russia. That RFP resulted in the invention of *the can* by Nicolas Appert in 1809. It helped feed his army. Canned food also enabled mariners to travel wide and far and for long periods. But the lead seams in cans drove artic mariners mad. GPS navigation was purely military before 1960 and is now a technology on which nearly all drivers depend. Night vision and ballistic missiles came out of Germany around 1940. Now, these are standard tools for hunters and serve to deliver supplies for astronauts in space stations. The idea of drones, crewless aerial vehicles, dates back to the 1850 period when the Austrians used the balloon to bomb Venice. During WWI, drones served as targets for artillery practice. By the year 2000, drones replaced some pilots, and in 2014, the FAA approved their operation for pipeline operations, and now Amazon makes home deliveries via drones. In civilian hands, drones can deliver illegal drugs, or deliver girl scout cookies, and also swarm to interrupt air traffic. Up to this point, military technology transfers have been mostly benign. Voluntary- and mandatory ethics mechanisms must be in place for the next wave of military Artificial Intelligence to be commercialized.

We are making progress when the following trends are strengthened:

When humans gain control over Artificial Intelligence technology, this is unlikely to happen at one big cataclysmic moment. It may happen in tiny increments, like private business citizens organizing for voluntary action, as outlined earlier, two NGOs practicing ethical standards and opposing abuse, respectively. Those NGOs will support governmental regulators to improve the law itself and provide continuous enforcement. Humans, that is many diverse humans, should sit on the control buttons of technology. An ethics vacuum may be the first step in a downward spiral into serfdom.

When the maximization of returns of investments does not eclipse caring for other humans. Saving money or making money with the AI does not have to come at anybody's expense. Henry Ford knew that paying good wages enabled workers to buy his cars. A technology that has the ability serve corporations well, must also serve their customers well.

When leading technology firms and venture funds become less powerful than democratic governments. Regulation has to step in and restore a balance that favors the population. Industry-developed – and government-enforced ethics standards are a remedy. The goal is to oblige the industry to recognize a moral framework of responsibility.

When the working class becomes the elite. As machines and algorithms take over human mental and physical labor, the full-time employed workforce is likely to shrink. The upper class will be composed of those who create, while the lower class will live comfortably on Universal Income and odd jobs. A role reversal with unknown effects which may be a mixed blessing.

When the private sector becomes the victim. Internet blackmail, ransoms, extortions, denial of service is approaching a revenue level large enough to be a new industrial sector. When abuse is State sponsored, it is not different than an old-fashioned declaration of war.

When democratic governments coordinate corporate taxation in response to rampant corporate tax-avoidance. This appears like a reasonable solution but raises constitutional questions. In the US, as elsewhere, taxation is linked to representations, not international agreements. Ethically, one must also recognize that nations compete among themselves, as do companies. Some nations just happen to be more efficient than others, and all have understandably different needs of service to their people.

All previous generations have faced industrial ethics challenges and they have either succeeded or they have failed to rise to a solution. We, The People, face technological ethics challenges to which we can either rise and thrive, or ignore and suffer.

The likelihood of a benevolent, wise person to assume the leadership and rescue all of us from Artificial Intelligence abuse is improbable. It would even be dangerous because such persons tend to remain neither benevolent nor wise. However, history has shown that small groups can start process and succeed on a national and global levels with amazing effects. Quoting Woody Allen, "all you have to do in life is to show up!"

Imagining a future spokesperson of Artificial Intelligence-empowered technologies addressing the UN's General Assembly may sound irrational, Still, this scenario is far better than having their voices excluded. So, where are we today?

- The information technology industry has all the money; they know it, and act accordingly with all manner of challenges.

- The regulators have the power to enforce any regulation they manage to write into law. Imposing penalties is lucrative and another form of paying for other programs.

- Citizens are by-standers and distrust both regulators and industry.

This is not just a local trend; it is present in Communist China as it is in the United States. In China there is the case of Alibaba v Xi Jinping, and in the United States in the case of the House of Representatives v the former Facebook. What then are the interest of the parties in conflict?

The industry looks for competitive advantage, income, and share price

The regulators need to get re-elected on popular issues like technological hype

The people look for stability, security, and a better future for the next generation

Graphically, the solution looks like this:

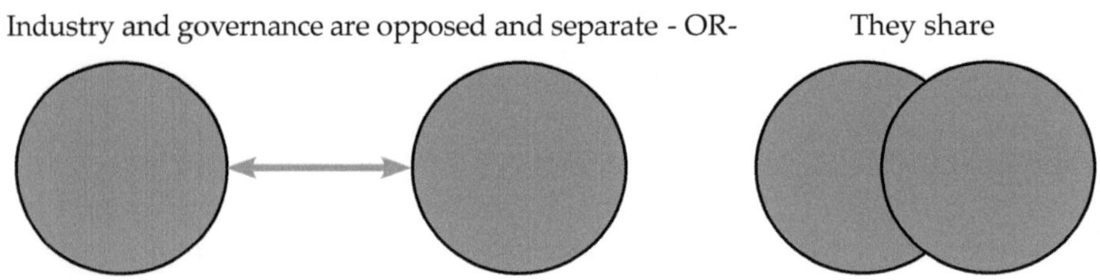

Figure 11.1

We, The People, who vote and spend money, suggest sharing governance of new technologies to jointly provide stability now for our future. For that, the industry needs an invitation to take a responsible seat at the table.

CHAPTER 12
FOURTEEN POINTS

Artificial Intelligence comprises a growing body of knowledge from many disparate frameworks. The word "consilience" means agreement among approaches to a topic, and it best describes this phenomenon. But the term does not help understand how to put it all together and begin to make sense. Grasping for an historical reference to insurmountable human problems, Woodrow Wilson came to mind. On January 8th, 1918, Woodrow Wilson, the 28th President of the United States, introduced Fourteen Points at the Versailles Peace Conference.

The human catastrophe was the end of World War One and simultaneously the crumbling of colonialism. One of those Versailles fourteen points was any nations' right to self-determination, based on their shared and unique cultures, languages, and history. The idea of self-determinism resonated at the beginning of the 20th Century with an exhausted world population awakening to declining colonialism. The conference also was an opportunity for countries to annex more territory justified by self-determinism. While Wilson's League of Nations failed, some of his ideas prevailed in the United Nations Charter. For the case of ethical technologies, fourteen is just a number. The hope is that one or more of the following fourteen points will take hold and lead to a promising future for people. When the advertising industry was concentrated on Madison Avenue in New York City, the creative types in Westport- Connecticut, had an insider expressing for testing innovative ideas. That expression was "put it on the train and see if it gets off in Westport'. So, let us set the following fourteen points into motion and see where they get off?

The Fourth Industrial Revolution, which includes the technologies of Artificial Intelligence, is coming at us fast and furiously. Its expected effects on society are as existential as the end of the WWI peace settlement was during Wilson's time. The difference is that we, unlike the WWI citizens, are not all exhausted, and we have the means to plan for better outcomes. It is a stretch, but self-determination and self-regulation have at least the word "self" in common.

The analogy is this: Wilsons' 14 Points resonated with nations and created hope for global peace.

The proposed 14 points start in the private/public sector to introduce ethics principles for powerfully new technology. The hard choices facing society are whether or not the Fourth Industrial Revolution's controlling effects, especially Artificial Intelligence, is to automate human work to the extent it replaces the human with algorithms and robots and turns humans into meta-world zombies? The answer is that we need to figure out both what to prevent and what to promote. We need to invent new design principles for Artificial Intelligence; design principles that anticipate the oncoming technology "freight train" and prepare workers before the total change takes hold. The early design stages of AI projects involving all stakeholders, workers, and the public, require a smooth transition. Training workers for new tools and new careers early in the process can prevent social upheaval.

And now to the fourteen points by which we aim to keep revolutionary technologies under human control and within ethical boundaries.

Point One

Self/co-Regulation entails the risk of failing, just as the Versailles Peace Conference in 1919 was not true to its stated intentions. President Wilson's concepts of self-determination created much hope for oppressed peoples after WWI. But as practiced at the time, the colonial powers' self-interest feeding frenzy to carve up the world among the winners was the net result. More than one hundred years later, the scars from mismanagement are still visible in the Middle East. Long-term effects the current generation fails to address may be painful for the next generation. Suppose self/co-regulation of Artificial Intelligence technologies fails due to the inevitable conflict with financial goals? In that case, the resulting scars on human well-being may still be visible one hundred years from now. Humans may have moved closer to being living automatons as we move deeper into Internet-empowered meta-verses. Doom co-exists with hope because 21st Century consumers are not a helpless class. Therein lies the difference between Versailles and now. Self/co-regulating new technologies on ethical standards call for careful execution.

Point Two

To err is human is a well-known expression and a quotation from Alexander Pope (1688-1744). Consider three scenarios, (a) when a small group of enormously powerful humans errs, they tend to err big; good intentions notwithstanding. In addition, the powerful elites are timid when it comes to corrections should they ever make a mistake? For example, Deng Xiaoping forced Communist China's one-child policy in 1979 with devastating effects and clear ethical violations in its practice. Ethical lapses also happen on a smaller scale. The customary non-disclosure of medical errors is just one example of bureaucracies practicing self-protection through imprecision. The phrase " when in doubt mumble" is a fair description of this phenomenon. For ethics in Artificial Intelligence to work, we do not have the luxury of time to get started defining it with standards. Getting started includes making public error corrections fast, but without punishing those who try in good faith and fail. That suggests working with large committees and making errors.

Point Three

Do No Harm is a well-known expression. The term is part of the Hippocratic Oath medical doctors take to deal ethically with their patients. In medicine, *doing no harm* is an established rule, but not in technology. That is because the economic incentives may come with a disadvantage to others, unquestionably competitors. The Google motto "don't be evil" is probably an adaption of the Hippocratic Oath to information technology. Without a good definition of the word "evil," the concept is vague. We can always defer to Supreme Court Justice Steward Potter, who in 1964 described the threshold for obscenity by " I know it when I see it." Applied to Artificial Intelligence, we know harm when we see it. Problem solved!

Point Four

Competition v Cooperation: The notion that competition can lead to good results is evident. Once a winner has taken it all, human nature kicks in, and exploitation is easy. Among technologists we say, "he who owns the robots and owns the data, will rule the world" is the fear of our time. That is competition, but the resources don't have to be in the hands of a small group. The co-operation that helped develop a vaccine in less than a year, while competition otherwise continued, is an example of capitalism in an ethical form. The point is that cooperation can and does produce value. Adopting standards for Artificial Intelligence in an environment of collaboration is the core message and path forward.

Point Five

Caring is exhibiting a concern for others, where "others" are people, institutions, environment, and society, to mention a few. The responsibility to care starts and ends with management at all levels in all organizations. For the private and public sectors, the term *caring* falls into the rubric of social responsibilities. Most enterprises have addressed social responsibility but need to revisit that theme as the technology advances, and the term *caring* takes on an enhanced nuance.

Point Six

Ground Rules for technological ethics already exist. The ethical intent is to find them and apply them. Chapter 5 is an excellent place to start. We are not lost sheep wandering an ethics minefield; we have benefitted dramatically from the history of human thought and past technological revolutions! The implication for today is that we can do it again; find old ground rules and fit them to our needs. As technology changes in many unpredictable ways, adjustments to existing regulations and developing new ones are the way to continue and remain in control.

Point Seven

Error Correction is the real strength of democracy and technology. Centralized, authoritarian planning managers look like geniuses as long as the outcomes are good. The positives of central planning, however, are not sustainable forever. Self/co-regulation of this new technology is a correction mechanism before the damages become catastrophic. Making policy errors is almost unavoidable and not always a sign of malintent or incompetence. It takes patience to live in an imperfect world.

Point Eight

Plan for a new social order to evolve naturally instead of designing a new social order from scratch, as if that were possible. Let us define social order as a connected system where parts of society work in unison to reach a new status quo. The current social order is modified capitalism, and the previous one was feudalism. Change is messy and often preceded by chaos. At present, we are in a state of early confusion preceding the coming 4th Industrial Revolution and have to prepare for the best possible chaos survival strategy. A plan must not only tell us what to do to survive well, but it must also say what not to do. Core structures like the family have to be supported and not undermined by technology.

Point Nine

Monopoly is the effective control of a resource that leads to unethical conduct and occurs intentionally and accidentally. Monopoly can be the result of spectacularly successful competition. (point 4). Even Adam Smith (1723 – 1790) in *Wealth of Nations* (1776) defined capitalism as land, labor, capital without monopoly. Monopoly would prevent the benefit of capitalism's invisible hand. Monopolies produce inefficiencies in the form of high prices and low growth. At the start of the Fourth Industrial Revolution, we find information to be the new oil. Information monopoly may lead to the creation of new classes among the population. The class with information can manipulate those without information. What used to be a land-owing aristocracy is now an information-controlling investment class. Emerging information monopolies are MAFIA+G, composed of Microsoft, Apple, Facebook, IBM, Amazon, and Google. In China, a similar group is called BAT, composed of Baidu, Alibaba, and Tencent. The power to control comes from making more money than their governments and influencing nearly all aspects of human life.

Point Ten

Happiness. As stated in the US Declaration of Independence, any human has inalienable rights to life, liberty, and the pursuit *of happiness.* That statement is globally accepted and no longer a US-centered value. That statement only guarantees the quest for happiness, not the achievement of happiness. However, technology should help and not hinder the pursuit of happiness.

Point 11

Transparency in Artificial Intelligence means that applications and their owners fully explain intent in simple day-to-day language. If done well, that creates trust; and trust, in turn, supports business success. The scientific method is an example where data support observations, measurements support conclusions, and testing leads to accept or fail for new theories until something better comes along. For example, breast cancer diagnoses utilizing Artificial Intelligence are now as accurate as those of an average medical diagnostician. For that to be transparent, the patients are entitled to know all surrounding facts and odds.

Point 12

An ethics vacuum for Artificial Intelligence exists because the technology is relatively new. If left alone, this issue will create insurmountable problems very soon. Karl Polonyi (1886–1964), a Hungarian economist, argued that transformative economic systems would eventually destroy themselves unless constrained. Unconstrained economies can flourish at the cost of something else, like the environment or the rights of people. When nations transitioned from a craft economy where workers were paid by the piece and worked in shops to a mass-production economy where people were paid hourly for working in factories, institutions called the shots. Such institutions were guilds, unions, and corporations. In the current digital economy, comparable institutions are the MAFIA+G (see Point Nine). In an unconstrained Artificial Intelligence ethics vacuum, technology can flourish at the expense of humans. That is very easy to do by giving people free stuff in return for data. The result is an obedient consumer and a meta-zombie. Polonyi, by the way, argued against self-regulation, for which we can forgive him. One hundred years ago, the word had a somewhat different meaning. It referred to large national economies rather than emerging technologies.

Point 13

Rights refer to the many human rights currently in the literature. Some of those came up in Chapter 5. The objective remains the same from the beginning of this book. The purpose is to enable this new technology to work for people, strengthen democracy and a free market, and shape a business culture under which good things can organically happen. In tabulating human rights on a grand scale and stipulation what to do about these, one is likely to encounter instances that are hard to enforce or even hard to define. Different cultures in the world have their own tolerances for rights. It may be easier to stipulate what is ethically taboo and go from there and then figure out what is allowed.

Point 14

Courage to conquer fear and make AI- ethics history. "The only thing we have to fear is fear itself " (Roosevelt's inaugural speech 1932). We have little choice but to overcome the nay-sayers among us, adapt to new technologies, and engineer ethical standards that help all people. Winston Churchill once said that "success is not final, and failure is not fatal."

Supporting the development of Artificial Intelligence technologies requires a new set of leaders to arise now. Leaders who can think big, leaders who remain independent, and leaders who will engineer strategies for ethical standards that work in the decades of rapid change. That is a tall practical order to follow, and it is a lot more than just doing good. Learn from our past to make the future.

NOTES AND REFERENCES

Chapter 1. Welcome to Industrial Revolutions

Asimov, I, (1950). *I-Robot,* Random House: New York.

Duljevic, V., Sattler, S., Racine, E. (2018). *Deciphering moral intuition: how agents, deeds, and consequences influence moral judgement,* PLOS/ONE, https://doi.org/10.1371/journal.pone/0204631.

Davenport, Thomas, (2019), *What does an AI Ethicist do?* MIT Sloan Management Review, June 24, 2019

Kissinger, H. A.(2018). *How the Enlightenment Ends.* The Atlantic, June 2018.

Nilson, J (2009, Stanford University), *The Quest for Artificial Intelligence, A History of Ideas and Achievements,* http://cambridge.org/us/

Russell, S. , Norvig P. (2017). *Artificial Intelligence,* Pearson.

Russell, S.(2019). *Human Compatible,* Viking.

Chapter 2 Which Ethical Framework? Pick one!

Brookings, *The EU Path towards regulation on artificial intelligence,* TechTank, April 26, 2021.

Business Roundtable (2019). *Corporate Governance,* August 19, 2019.

California Assembly Bill 459 (2019). www.info.legislature.ca.gov

European Commission, (2020), *White Paper on Artificial Intelligence,* a *European approach to excellence and trust,* COM (2020) 65 final February 19, 2020

https://www.finra.org/rules-guidance/key-topics/fintech/report/artificial-intelligence-in-the-securities-industry/overview-of-ai-tech

General Data Protection Regula (2018), *European law,* http://en.wikipedia.org/wiki/General_Data_Protection_Regulation.

Kak, Amba ed (2020), *Regulating Biometrics, Global Approach and Urgent Questions,* AiNow Institute, September 1, 2020

Office of the Attorney General.(2019).*California Consumer Privacy Act, CCPA Fact Sheet*, Office of the attorney, www.oag.ca.gov/privacy/ccpa

Proposed e-Privacy Regulation, (2017). The National Law Review, 12/11/2017, http://www.gtlaw.com/en/insights.

Standish, T., (2019) *Regulating AI*, The Economist-The World in 2019, p24

UK Government (2018), *AI Report, Parliament(UK), (2018), AI in UK, Ready Willing and Able*, CM9645.

Universal Declaration of Human Rights,(1948) United Nations Dept of Public Information, DPL876. rev, 1988

UNRSID (2004), *Research and Policy Brief 1, Social Responsibility, and Business Regulation*, www.unrsid.org

Wikipedia, *California Consumer Privacy Act*. http://en.wikipedia.org/w/index.php?

Chapter 3 Role Models for Self-Regulation already exist

FINRA, https://www.finra.org

https://www.finra.org/rules-guidance/key-topics/fintech/report/artificial-intelligence-in-the-securities-industry/key-challenges

ISO, https://www.iso.org

US Department of Labor, (2009), *Reflections on OSHA's History*, https://www.osha.gove/history.

Chapter 4 The Case for Starting with Self-Regulation First

Ammanath, B et al., (2020), *Thriving in the era of pervasive AI. Deloitte's State of AI in the enterprise*, 3rd edition, July 14, 2020.

Coman, A. et al, (2018), *AI Rebel Agent*, AI Magazine, Fall 2018doi.

Berger, B., (2019), *The (updated) purpose of the US Corporation*, The Wall Street Journal, https://blogs.wsj.com,/cio/2019/08/30/the-updated-purpose-of-the-corporation.

Davenport, T, (2019), *What does an ethicist do?* MIT Sloan Management Review, June 24, 2019.

Gunningham, N., Rees, J.,(2020), *Industry Self-Regulation: An Institutional Perspective*, doi/epdf/10.1111/1467-9930-101, July 18, 2020.

https://www.finra.org/rules-guidance/key-topics/fintech/report/artificial-intelligence-in-the-securities-industry/ai-apps-in-the-industry

IBM, (2019), *precision legislation*, policy blog https://www.ibm.com/blogs/policy/facial-recognition/

Kearns, M., Roth, A.,(2020). *Ethical algorithm design should guide technology regulation*, Brookings Institution, Washington DC: January 13, 2020.

McCarthy, M. (2020), *AI Needs more regulation, not less*, Brookings AI governance series, https://www.brookings.edu/research/ai-needs-more-regulation-not-less.

Norman, W. (2011) *Business Ethics as Self-regulation*, Journal of Business Ethics, Springer.

Ouchychy, L, Coin, A., Dubljevic, V., (2020). *AI in the headlines: the portrayal of ethical issues of Artificial Intelligence in the media*, Open Forum:https://doi.org/10.1007/s00146-020-00965-5.

West, D., (2018) *The role of corporations in addressing AI's ethical dilemmas*, Brookings Institution: Sept 2018, http://www.brookings.edu.

Wiens, J. et al., (2019), *Do No Harm: a roadmap for responsible machine learning for health care*, Springer: Nature Medicine, August 29, 2029.

Chapter 5 What to Regulate, that is the Ethics Question

Brookings, *The EU Path towards regulation on artificial intelligence*, TechTank, April 26, 2021.

Business Roundtable (2019). *Corporate Governance*, August 19, 2019.

California Assembly Bill 459 (2019). www.info.legislature.ca.gov. Fact Sheet

California Department of Justic, California *Consumer Privacy Act*

European Commission, (2020), *White Paper on Artificial Intelligence, a European approach to excellence and trust*, COM (2020) 65 final February 19, 2020

FINRA,(2020), *Artificial Intelligence in the Security Industry*, https://www.finra.org/rules guidance/key topics/fintech/report/artificial-intelligence-in-the-securities-industry/overview-of-ai-tech

General Data Protection Regulation (2018), *European law*, http://en.wikipedia.org/wiki/General_Data_Protection_Regulation.

Kerns, Michael, et al., (2020) *Ethical algorithms should guide technology regulations*. Brookings, January 13, 2020.

MacCarthy, Mark (20200, *AI Needs more regulation, not less*. Brookings, March 9, 2020.

Mathews, K., Bowman, C. (2018). *California Consumer Privacy Act*, Proskauer Privacy Law Blog, July 13, 2018

Office of the Attorney General.(2019).*California Consumer Privacy Act, CCPA Fact Sheet*, Office of the attorney, www.oag.ca.gov/privacy/ccpa

Proposed e-Privacy Regulation, (2017). The National Law Review, 12/11/2017, http://www.gtlaw.com/en/insights.

Standish, T., (2019) *Regulating AI*, The Economist-The World in 2019, p 24.

Stanford Encyclopedia of Philosophy, *Principle of Beneficence in Applied Ethics*, ISSS1095-5054, Metaphysics Lab.

UK Government (2018), *AI Report, Parliament(UK), (2018), AI in the UK, Ready Willing and Able*, CM9645.

Universal Declaration of Human Rights,(1948) United Nations Dept of Public Information, DPL876. rev, 1988

UNRSID (2004), *Research and Policy Brief 1, Social Responsibility, and Business Regulation*, www.unrsid.org

Wladawsjy, I, (2019), *The (Updated) Purpose of the US Corporation*, Wall Street Journal, https://wsj.com/cio/2019/08/30/the-updated-purpose-of-the-corporation/

Chapter 6 Ethics Self-Regulation in Practice

Abbott, R. (2020) *It is time to rethink the legal treatment of robots*, MIT Technology Review, October 22, 2020.

Blackman, R, A (2020) *Practical guide to building ethical AI*, Technology and Innovation an HBR email newsletter, October 15, 2020.

Dublijevic V, et al (2018), *Deciphering Moral Intuition; How agents, deeds, and consequences influence moral judgment,* PLoS1,13(10):e2044.

Hutson, Mathew, (2021), *Who Should Stop Unethical AI,* Annals of Technology, February 15, 2021.

Bryan, J., (2020) *How do you teach a machine right from wrong*? National Post, June 6, 2019.

FINRA, https://www.finra.org/rules-guidance/key-topics/fintech/report/artificial-intelligence-in-the-securities-industry/key-challenges

Kak, A., (2020) *Regulating Biometrics,* AINOW, September 2020.

Kim, T, Mejia, S, (2019) *From Artificial Intelligence to Artificial Wisdom, What Socrates Teaches US,* Computer, IEEE Computer Society, doi 10.1109/MC 2019-2929733.

Klein, A., (2020), *Reducing bias in AI-based financial services,* Brookings, Brookings Institution, Washington DC, July 10, 2020.

Lucas, E. (2018), *Tech Giants must come clean with customers,* The Times, London, August 31, 2018.

Martin, L. 2018, *Learn from History and do not blindly trust,* The Times, London, August 28, 2018.

Meissner, G., (2020) *Artificial Intelligence: Consciousness and conscience,* AI and Society, Springer, 35:225-235, https://doi.org/10.1007/s00146-019-00880-4.

Stanford University, (2019), *The concept of beneficence and benevolence,* Stanford Encyclopedia of Philosophy, ISSN 1095-5054.

The Economist, (2020) *Testing the Faith* (Charlemagne – on privacy), April 25, 2020, p 44.

Chapter 7 Re-Engineering our Common Future

European Commission, *White Paper, On Artificial Intelligence – A European Approach to Excellence and Trust,* COM(2020) 65 Final

Testing the Faith (of privacy), The Economist, April 25th, 2020.

Kim, T.W., Mejia ,S, (2019), *,From Artificial Intelligence to Artificial Wisdom: What Socrates teaches us.* Computers,

Chapter 8 Measuring Ethics

Wolf, F.(2020), *Performance Measurements in the Age of Artificial Intelligence,* Bookboon, London UK, 2020.

Zuboff, Shoshana,(2019) *The Age of Surveillance Capitalism,* Public Affairs, New York, 2019

Chapter 9 The Next Level – Quantum Computing

Jackson, M., (2017), *Six things quantum computers will be incredibly useful for,* http://singularityhub.com

Microsoft (2020), *Introduction to quantum computing and the quantum development kit-QDK.* https://docs.microsoft.com/en/us/quantum/overview/overview Singularity Hub,

The Economist, (2020), *Uncertainty Principals,* The Economist: September 26, 2020, p.72.

Singularity Hub, *Things Quantum Computers will be Incredibly Useful For,* https:singularityhub.com/2017/06/25/6.

The Economist, (2020), *Uncertainty Principles,* September 26, 2020.

Wikipedia, www.wikipedia.com/quantum computing.

Chapter 10 Regulatory Challenges

Gupta, A, Health V. (2020), *AI Ethics Groups are repeating one of society's classic mistakes,* MIT Technology Review, September 14, 2020

Standage, Tom (2019), *Regulating Artificial Intelligence,* The World 2119 (The Economist)

Chapter 11 Regulatory Trends

Brean, Joseph, (2019), *How do you teach a machine right from wrong?* National Post, June 6, 2019.

IBM, *Bold Ideas for a digital Society,* http://ibm.com./blogs/policy/facial-recognition/

Kahneman, Daniel, Silbony, Oliver, Sunstein, Cass. *The Capitalist Culture that Built America,* The Wall Street Journal, May 15-16, 2021, C3.

MacCarthy, Mark, (2020), *AI needs more Regulation, not less.* Brookings 9 March, (2020), https://brookings.edu/research/ai-needs-more-regulation-not-less/

Pandya, J.,(2019) *Troubling Trends towards Artificial Intelligence Governance,* Forbes: February 25, 2019.

Pentland, A. et al., *Time for a New Digital Bretton Woods,* Barrons, June 21, 2021

Pop V. et al. *From Lightbulbs to 5G, China Battles West for Control of Vital Standards,* Wall Street Journal, February 8, 2021.

Chapter 12 Fourteen Points

Kochan, Thomas A., (2021), *Artificial Intelligence and the Future of Work: A Proactive Strategy,* AI Magazine, Spring 2021, 42:1, p. 16

MacMillan, Margaret, *Paris 1919,* Random House, New York, 2001.

ABOUT THE AUTHOR:

The author's career path spans engineering, coding, corporate management, a White House fellowship, pro bono public service in local government, starting and operating a business, and teaching MBA students. From the combination of practicing bare knuckles business to inspiring business students, and together with an interest in human history, emerged this book. It addresses the need to understand mankind's unpreparedness for the technologies of the 4th industrial revolution. Frank Wolf is an arbitrator/mediator for FINRA and contributor to technology ethics studies

Dr. Wolf now lives in Asheville, North Carolina, USA, and can be reached at *frkwlf@gmail.com.*

www.ingramcontent.com/pod-product-compliance
Ingram Content Group UK Ltd.
Pitfield, Milton Keynes, MK11 3LW, UK
UKHW041644031026
15587UKWH00001B/479

9 781871 891737